Dear P&O
Firstly, I'd like to call you Pa
more personal, tho my apol(
:-)
Myself and my beautiful wife have recently arrived home from a simply wonderful cruise, my wife has never felt so relaxed on a holiday she has told me, this is fantastic, but unfortunately comes with its own troubles, which I'll come to later. We were on cruise N120, aboard the magnificent Ventura, what an incredible thing, much better than my Aldi inflatable dinghy (took me 3 hours to inflate by mouth at my local reservoir, the supplied pump broke after 2 pumps !!!), the obligatory impulse buy when browsing the middle aisle whilst the wife is looking for the beans to feed the kids (we were saving for a cruise). I've suggested that Aldi send these dinghies to France, the clandestine won't even get off the beach :-)... sorry, I'm side-tracking...
The reason I am making contact is to offer a few pointers/recommendations, hopefully you'll take on board (if you'll pardon the pun) :-)
The boarding process first. Obviously we are now under a new way of doing things, and I'm absolutely satisfied with your way of doing things, it was pretty good, a few things need tweaking, I'm sure this will come with time. It did feel like I was an extra in E.T The Extra Terrestrial, the bit where he's been found almost dead (I thought he was, cried my eyes out) where the scientist's erect their tents and mobile laboratory. My suggestion would be some nice hanging baskets (not from Home Bargains, they don't last) and some piped music (not Celine Dion

tho, we don't want " My Heart Will Go On " at this point, maybe " Sailing " by good ol Rod Stewart ") . This will hopefully set a more tranquil zone, and help us relax before the nasal probe.

Now we get to onboard. The first thing I noticed was how long the corridors are. They may well be great for Usain Bolt wannabes, but no fun for me, dragging 3 x hand luggage bags, 2 suits, 6 dresses and 3 tubes of pringles (2 salt and vinegar, 1 ready salted) (the tubes make a great pretend telescope if you put a black sock over them first, look ace at sail away). My suggestion would be a travelator, like at airports, not the gladiator's one (though I always thought I'd be able to do that one, even with Wolf and Hunter at the top, giving it the big en).

The cabin now. We were in a cabin with a window, partially obstructed with a lifeboat. All perfect, though a few warning signs need prominently placing in the room. No.1 A warning that every other day, the lifeboats are cleaned/serviced, therefore, those carrying out the cleaning/servicing have a great view into your cabin. I never take my temperature orally, and it's easier on all fours naked.

No.2, try to avoid the toilet when crossing the Bay Of Biscay, it's notoriously choppy, it's easy to slip, and there's no nail brush supplied.

No.3, similar to No.2, this time, no getting frisky when on Bay Of Biscay, it's very easy to slip, and people are not thankful at all. I was left limping for 2 day's :-)

Dining now. Whilst I appreciate the finer things in life, especially real butter, I'd suggest you don't serve it laced with kryptonite, I bent at least 4 knives and destroyed at least 3 loaves of bread. I have also ruined 2 t-shirts, got stains under the armpits where I tried, to no avail, to soften it (the all new Daz with stain remover is a lie, it doesn't work, I'll be messaging them next) . I'd suggest that you serve "I can't believe it's not butter (it's now back to that name, they changed it to " I can't believe it's so good for everything " but reverted back thanks to my email) or Utterly Butterly. Clover is good, but not currently on offer at Asda, the other 2 are. If you are to continue serving real butter, then leave it in the theatre on board a few hours before serving, it's like an oven in there.

Your " clotted cream " is not, in any way, shape or form " clotted cream ", at best it's dream topping. It may well be " clotted cream " in the supplemented restaurant's, but I'm not " made of money "... the jams are nice tho :-)

Don't call it " jus ", call it gravy, saves lots of explanation to those who come from the North, " jus " is fine in the aforementioned supplemented restaurants.

Butterscotch Angel Delight would be a welcome addition :-)

Make the custard with milk, not water, spoilt a few good crumbles with it, tastes like rainwater.

Entertainment now.

On the whole, very good. I'd like some binoculars in the theatre, like the little ones at the local hippodrome's, that way I can accurately rate the dancers out of 10, I could only manage a high score of 8, the 2 pringles tubes taped together didn't do anything (tho the salt and vinegar in my eyes was no fun).

The quizzes are great fun, but a world cruise as a prize is far more appealing than a glass, as nice as they are, tho I didn't even win one of them :-(

During our cruise, the ppv boxing was on, it would have been most excellent getting to see " The Gypsy King " beat " The Bronze Bummer ". It would also have helped me shed a few lbs, as I'd no doubt be shadow boxing like " Rocky " whilst listening to " Eye Of The Tiger " on my Dr Dre Beats (there actually my son's, they are real tho, not from the car boot) for the remainder of the cruise.

On shore trips...

Absolutely loved them, my favourite was Lisbon. But, for the love of God, please don't make us do the zig zag marathon when disembarking and embarking, I may well be sub 10 seconds down the corridor to my room (Usain Bolt I'm after you) but I'm no Mo Farah.

So now onto the troubles after.

On arrival home, none of my kids had cleared the dog shit from the decking !!!

The bins hadn't been emptied !!!

The plant's hadn't been watered !!!

And apparently, the blinds weren't opened correctly !!!

A final note ....

I have to make my bed myself every morning !!!

Think I need another cruise. So if Pamela or Oswald read this, private message me with any free cruise you may wish to send us / me on, or discount code for a future sailing :-)

See you onboard in the near future, that is if my backs OK, I'm writing this from A and E, had to go back to bloody work, put my back out, another pitfall of time off lol

Take care Mark & Helena

O, one more... Apparently fridge magnets are not an appropriate gift for teenagers, especially when there's Pandora and a watch shop on board !!!

And their reply......

Hi Mark, firstly, were glad you and your wife had a wonderful time on board and we're so happy you and your 3 tubes of Pringles were able to join us (great choice of snack btw and a great use of an empty tube however, we would never recommend using the salt and vinegar ones for binoculars, be careful!). Your comments regarding the crew cleaning and warnings in the rooms have been noted. However you wish to take your temperature is up to you and we agree this should be done in complete privacy, considering your preference. The Bay Of Biscay, can cause us to become a little rocky so, we urge you to be more careful in future. We don't want any injuries! Softer butter and butterscotch angel delight, noted. Not sure we can pop to Asda but, we'll certainly make the ship aware of your efforts in trying to simply spread butter on your dinner roll. We're glad you enjoyed the entertainment on board. We're not sure a world cruise can be considered as a quiz prize but, you never know what will be offered in the future! Across the fleet we have Sport 24 which offers coverage of many sporting events. We can only apologise that you were not able to watch the fight, meaning shadow boxing in preparation was out of the question. We completely take responsibility for a couple of those lbs not lost. However, we hope the longer corridors and zig zags at disembarkation helped. That said, you could always blow up the dinghy now your home, this might burn a few calories? Your choice of gifts sounds perfect to us and unfortunately, we cannot help with the full bins and mess of your decking you faced upon your return home. We can however guarantee that the next time you join us, we will look after you and make your bed whenever needed. We hope that you will both be able to join us on board again in the future and we cannot wait to welcome you back! Till next time… Best Wishes, Laura (not Pamela & Oswald) ●

Yo Pam (I assume you'll pick this up as Ozzy will be steering the ship)
I hope I find you well :-)
I'd like to hope you remember me :-) I'm the butter guy :-) (I hope you've replaced the knives I bent, and took up the " i can't believe it's
not butter " tip I gave you? , tho it's not currently on offer, i think it's Clover this week)
Well you'll be happy to know that I'll be boarding Ventura again on Tuesday 3rd May. I'm coming with my wife and

2 of my beloved kids, tho at 16 and 18, they're adults, not that they paid for themselves mind !!! They are, fundamentally, the reason I'm reaching out. You see, this trip was supposed to be just the Wife and I, to celebrate our 27th wedding anniversary that was Friday gone. I was in the process of booking when my Son kindly informed me that his passport was still in date, 2 years left to be precise, so I didn't need to leave him and his sister at home dog sitting, not that they'd have cleared the s@#t from the decking (I filled one of them JD bag's when I got back last time) .

This led me to book a family room, finance's wouldn't allow me 2 rooms or one of the posh suites. With that said, I'll not beat around the bush (or will I? ;-)) What's the chances of bagging a free upgrade? :-). I'm sure you can wangle something :-). I promise not to moan when the butter ruins my toast :-) . You'll also save me a few quid, as I won't then have to sample the delights on offer within Amsterdam ;-) (does anyone know if they accept credit card ?) the wife will be able to meet my needs :-) I shall of course offer something in return, maybe a cake or 3 from the special cafe's that line the wonderful canal lined streets, so long as you don't let Ozzy have one, I don't want the return journey to be like the Bay of Biscay, wife's still limping from my missed aim :-). You'll also be saving my kids from hearing me...... SNORE ... :-)

I'll wrap up now, got to watch the footy whilst wifey iron's and packs the cases, does the dinner and cleans the house from top to bottom, fingers crossed she'll see to the decking too :-)

Take care, happy sailings, I'll / we'll see you on board :-)
Love Mark, Helena and 2 of the Brady Bunch :-)
Foot note... Heron foods currently have utterly butterly
on special, short date, but will see this cruise sorted :-)

Last year I'd never cruised, next week I embark on my
3rd in 8 months :-) (sold my spleen to pay :-))
So as a seasoned cruiser, i now feel my inner " Jane
Mcdonald " and offer some insight and tips.....

Don't forget your masks, not essential now, I know, but I
watched Blue Peter as a kid, and took inspiration from
them, and made my wife a bikini from the ones we'd got
left over, saved me a few quid in Primark :-)
Another Blue Peter inspired build you can do on board is
the pringles binoculars/telescope, great for watching
dolphins, whales or the fitties at the pool/hot tub :-) , be
careful if using salt n vinegar, your eyes will sting for
day's after !!!
You need at least a 3 week cruise to attempt Tracey
Island, and double sided sticky tape :-)
Get at least 4 cobs/baps/barms/rolls at dinner, when
no.1, 2 and 3 are torn to shreds by the butter/kryptonite,
you'll have one left.
Take a hand held mini vacuum to clean up your mess
from the above.

When on sundeck, lean over the side, shout you can see whale's, you'll then have the pick of sunloungers as everyone rushes to see.

Men, upon your first arrival at the cabin, take the cases in, then leave your wife/significant other in the room, whilst you take both room cards without their knowledge with you to the bar/casino/burger bar, keep away for a few hours and the unpacking will be done.

Women, take note of above, upon their return, take both cards with you and enjoy the obscenely expensive shop's... that'll teach them.

Don't do your morning exercises/yoga naked on the balcony, apparently those above can see, and don't want to see what you had for dinner the previous night

Be careful on the toilet, especially across the Bay of Biscay, the toilet roll is not the best, and there's no nail brush.

Take a suit at least a size bigger, especially if your cruise is over a week long, you'll need it towards the end.

Don't attempt to make love whilst crossing the Bay of Biscay, accidents can and DO HAPPEN and will ruin learning to line dance.

Buy as much booze and as many fags/bakky as u can, once home you can carboot it, and you can triple your money, will help pay for all that was purchased by your significant other, it should, all being well cover the bill.

Don't bother with the WiFi, it's crap, tho I'd happily share someone's connection so I keep my wordle streak going :-)

Don't throw unwanted breakfast items over the side, Dolphins don't like croissants/toast/crunchy nut cornflakes (they can clearly resist them)
Don't use the corridor as a place to re-enact Usain Bolt's 2012 London Olympic Games gold, it's no fun running into someone exiting from room 5517, so close to the 100m mark too (sure I was sub 9 seconds)
Don't expect those you leave at home to have looked after the house, watered the plants and cleaned the dog poo from the decking, it's a nightmare to get out the cracks!!! (side tracking, but whatever happened to white dog poo ??? :-))

Look forward to seeing you all onboard :-)
25th June we embark :-) , I'll be the one with a black eye after my wife sees the bikini :-)

Day one ....
Off we go on virtuosa, our first MSC cruise 🚢, Me, the Mrs and the Obligatory teenager (17) who don't wanna stay at home, hoping that Marjorie, Sheila and Cressidia are as welcoming as Pam & Oswald :-). We set off at 9.30 from Brum, we had a boarding time of 2, so this allowed plenty of time, we knew the roads were to be busy due to the greedy "Thomas The Tankers" drivers strike, must be hard to cope on £60k !!!
After 5 minutes, 3 miles driving, with at least 3 " are we there yet " questions, we were needing to stop for the bog !! So we pull into the Services. Wife and I opted for tea and hot chocolate from Costa, son obviously required a Burger King, ordering a triple bacon cheese

burger meal (large), chicken fries (delicious, try if u haven't), complete with a coke, breakfast of champions and Geoff Capes !!! Luckily for me, no mortgage required as we have a discount for Moto services ●, if I hadn't, then a bush at the side of the hard shoulder would have been the bog, and they'd have had to make do with the sherbet lemons and polo's from the glove box (no werthers in there, I'm not that old yet) . As we left the services, I aquaplaned passing the fuel station, it hadn't been raining, it was the tears of those filling up when they got wind of the price per litre !!!! I'd been sensible, got some red diesel from a farmer, swapped it for rare pokemon card ●

Back on the motorway, about an hour passes, when wife informs me she hasn't packed a jacket !!! 20 pairs of flip flops made it, but no jacket. So we stopped off at Banbury, no sign of the " fair lady upon a white horse " ... there's a retail park tho, so some more "last minute" shopping is done, 6 dresses, 4 pairs of flip flops and a jacket 5 shop's later. Thankfully, the money I saved on the fuel covered the cost, may even have enough left for a new extention on the house.

Another 2 hours and we make it to the port, but not without perforated ear drums, thanks to the wife's screams of joy at seeing the ship. She is a beautiful thing tho, she's huge, and that's not man brag/exaggeration, she really is gargantuan.

Thankfully, this time around, there's no getting sticked up the nose with a cotton bud by the extras from E.T, so boarding is a pretty easy process, as long as you've printed off everything required, 4 cartridges, and 2 reams of paper we went through for the 3 of us, I'll claim it on my expenses 🌑 but we were on within 20 minutes. Onboard and WOW 🌑, she's magnificent, truly beautiful. Very opulent and bling. I, as did wifey and son, knew instantly we were gonna love it here :-)

Time now to find the cabin. Everything onboard is modern, and interactive, very Elon Musk, so great for techy types, but probably confusing for the oldies sailing. A couple of looks and playing about on the touch screens, we think we know the way. So we take the lift to deck 10 and make our way to our home for the next week.

Cabin found, and it's great, got a balcony, so perfect for dolphin 🐬 and whale spotting 🐋 if we're lucky. No cases as of yet, so we head off for some food and drink :-) . It's a marathon to the buffet, we're at the front of the ship, it's at the back, I was proper Hank Marvin, so I think I came close to Mo Farah's 2012 record time, tho having stuffed myself with a bit of everything, I'm not gonna be doing the " Mobot" on my return back to the cabin, well and truly stuffed, pizza the star of the buffet, and the butter, happy to report no " Uri Geller " knife bending, all being well, a trend ; I'm gonna be conducting BUTTER REPORT...

After lunch, it was unfortunately unpacking time, a job ordinarily undertaken by the wife, but she was already frequenting the onboard shop's, so it was up to me, a job done in record time, and no hanger

shortage here, didn't use a single one, managed to stuff everything into a couple of draws, so no idea why she spent the last week ironing :-) . Then I treated myself to a well earned nap, only to be rudely awakened by the wife's effing and blinding at me, apparently my unpacking effort was not up to scratch !!!! How ungrateful. ●

I calmed her down with an offer to buy her a nice handbag and purse combo this trip, there's a Primark at the Banbury retail park, and we got to pass by it upon our way home, and technically, we'll still be on our trip :-) Son went off to explore the ship, good job he's geared up, head to toe in North Face gear, it's gonna be expedition esq checking out everywhere, apparently if all the corridors were laid out straight, they'd stretch from the corner shop in "Open All Hours " to the North Pole ●

After the rearranged unpacking, it was time for evening meal, so we made our way down to the assigned restaurant for dinner. Can't lie, wasn't wowed by this, I had a chicken kiev, looked like a jiffy bag, tasted like the inside of an empty jiffy bag, bland as, and served with mash (I'm assuming potatoes) that tasted like my pillow in the morning, not even the (again acceptable) butter made a difference. Pudding alright tho, nice sticky toffee pudding.

With dinner done, we had a little mooch around and a drink, but as we were already tired, and knowing we had the arduous journey back to the room, we gave in and called it a night. On the way back, I laid a trail of bread stick crumbs (I'd sneaked a few out in my socks) so as to easily find our way back in the morning, a trick I'd seen Bear Grilles do in the South American Archipelago :-), only I won't have to repel from a helicopter, and I'll be

eating bacon and sausage and sipping orange juice, not rotten squirrel balls or the liquid squeezed from and elephants poo ....
Footnote will be butter watch, I'll be using a grading scale, hardest being Chuck Norris, softest George, the pink hippo from Rainbow
Breakfast :- N/A
Lunch :- Gary Barlow
Dinner :- Any strictly come dancing judge :-)

Day 2... sea day
Boy did I need that sleep 😴 woke up feeling fresh as a daisy :-) . Sea day today, so was time to dig out my North Face gear and explore this leviathan, unfortunately wife hadn't packed my karrimor hiking boots, so I had to make do with my sliders, I bet Sir Rannolph Finnes doesn't have this problem !!! They should be fine tho, I wore them when I did Everest, amazing place, best Nepalese restaurant ever :-)
Wasn't happy to find that the cleaners had vacuumed up my trail of bread stick crumbs, had to use my instinct, and follow the smell of bacon...left sleeping beauty in bed, just me and the son went, we made it there in around 2 hours, 29 minutes, so not to shabby, especially in sliders :-) . Only a few issues here, one will be noted in BUTTER REPORT, the other, my own fault, burnt me toe, dropped bean juice on it, so trainers tomorrow, sliders will be for pool trips only.
As I'm the perfect hubby, after my breakfast, I lovingly prepped (plated up) a nice selection for the wife, pancakes with syrup cooked banana 🍌 and a selection

of pastries, probably enough to feed the pigeons in Trafalgar Square, but she was very grateful :-) as will the seagulls and fish with the leftovers I lobbed overboard :-)

Brekky done, I ditched the hiking gear, and slipped into my football kit, well board shorts, t-shirt, odd socks and trainers, didn't want to be a FKW :-) . it was then off to the indoor sports hall. Obviously put my son in goal first so I could show him my free kick skills :-) I got him to line up a few of the kid's in there as a wall, and unleashed an absolute belter, right into a 6 year old little girls face, she wasn't even in the wall, she was happily eating ice-cream by the corner spot :-(I'm clearly no Messi anymore, and quickly left, as there were lots of Ger"s kit's present, didn't want Glaswegian handshake from an angry dad/mom ●

With the football done with, I now officially hang my boots up (no Ballon d'or) for good and for my safety, we decide on table tennis :-) . Can't believe how knackering even that is !! Won 2 out of 5 games, safe to say I'm no Forest Gump :-) told the son I LET him win ;-

Whilst we were being all sporty, wife went shopping with my Mom and Stepdad who joined us, to buy some duty free, fags were a bargain, should have no trouble shifting them on back home ● . We then met up and had lunch at the buffet together, again, plenty of choice, including a Sunday roast of beef and yorkies :-) Aunt Georgia or whatever the Italian equivalent to Aunt Bessie is...9

After dinner, wifey went back to the cabin for a nap whilst I went swimming with the boy, lovely and warm, but salty, assuming sea water and not my sweat residue :-?

After swimming, wife and I went to chill at the back of the boat, bit of sunbathing and drinks, whilst chatting to some lovely people, cruisers really are a great bunch, so friendly ⚫

Back to cabin for a shower, which was epic, really, refreshing, and changed into something smart for dinner. Dinner in the main restaurant was very good today, I had soup to start with, looked like dishwater, but tasted pretty good. Followed that with my son's carpaccio, he didn't know it was raw steak lol, it was nice :-) ... I then went for the Beef Wellington and a baked alaska for dessert. All perfectly acceptable this evening, hoping yesterday was a glitch. After dinner we had a chilled evening sampling some of the many cocktails on offer 🍸 sat watching the sea, managing to see a few dolphins, tho none of them were jumping like they do in SeaWorld 🐬 Unfortunately tho, i did see a fair few discarded masks, I know dolphins are smart, but i don't think they are protecting themselves from covid, so it's clearly some idiot discarding them into the sea...... in bed by 11, watched a bit of TV and then crashed out once son got in, he went and kept himself entertained ..... La Rochelle tomorrow, apparently it's not named after the pretty one from The Saturdays

Leaving the English Channel and it's merging with the Bay of Biscay was a little choppy, but no mishaps to leave wife limping this time, son is sharing our room, and she was washing her hair :-)

Butter Watch
Breakfast :- Tyson Fury
Lunch :- Phil Mitchell
Dinner :- Jack Grealish

Day 3....
Woken early this morning by loud rumbling, thought it was the sprouts the wife had at dinner making their presence known, but a quick (and brave) head dip under the quilt told me that my suspicion was wrong. It was the engine thrusts as we were docking into La Rochelle, our first port of call. Hopefully I've slept through the sprouts return :-)
Can't say I was impressed when I opened the curtains and stepped out onto the balcony for a gander, the beach was just a mass pile of sand, dumped onto a concrete slipway !!! Soon realised, when I went for brekky, that this was not the beach, it was likely just a source of building sand for the docks, there was a nice beach the opposite side of the ship ●
Just the Son and me for breakfast this morning, think the wife likes me spoiling her with it in bed, lazy ● more like it. Good selection again in the buffet, I kept it simple tho :- Bacon, sausage, eggs (fried, poached, boiled (don't like scrambled)) beans, black pudding, hash brown, corned beef hash (lovely this was) , 2 waffles, 3 cobs/barms/baps/rolls (call em what u will) , washed

down with a few cans of coke (diet obviously) 🐽. Took the wife a Crossiant and jam :-), she'd asked for eggs, but after getting lucky with the sprouts, I wasn't risking it, so told her they'd got none left :-)

Brekky done and dusted we thought about getting off the ship, but I'd heard the place was full of French people, so didn't bother, as not keen on them after they mauled us in the six nations and won it overall. Not a fan of snails and frogs legs either. I'll insert my apologies to any French onboard, especially if they also work for British Rail.

So the plan for the day was lounge by the pool. I placed our towels and gubbins over 27 beds, can't miss out on the best spot, and lathered myself in ambre solaire, donned my shades and planted myself. Just gotten comfortable when wife wanted me to rub oil into her. Under normal circumstances, if she asks me to oil her up, I'm on it like a tramp on chips, but just rubbing it into her back ain't quite the same ;-) . Got back to the sunbathing and had a go at the " guess the smile quiz " they did on the big screen, getting a respectable 13 out of 15 correct :-) the 2 wrong ones were wife's answers of course :-). Afternoon soon arrived and we indulged in a little bit of lunch, a couple slices of pizza 🍕 , its very good, and some nuggets and chips :-) and some suckling pig, I was certain she'd stayed by the pool :-). After dinner I set up my camera, above the main pool area to capture a time-lapse of the goings on, tho wife kept making me paranoid, saying someone would nick the camera, thankfully they didn't, and if I do another, don't be tempted too, as it's tracked, and I once did a karate lesson so I'm hard as nails :-) video tuned out great, tho I didn't manage to capture any " you've been framed moment's, £500 per video they pay now, so if anyone sees my set up again, fall down the stairs or pretend a shark/crocodile is attacking you, I'll split the prize money 75/25 :-)

Had a half hour swim which was nice, then back to the room to freshen up for the evening.

Down for dinner at 6.30, and decided to pass on the main restaurant and just slum it in the buffet. There was so much choice tonight, including some cooked fresh for you, bbq style pork chops and chicken thighs, they were banging, so I attacked that and the whole buffet like food was going out of fashion, I reckon I'd have given @Leah Shutkever (if u know, u know) a run for her money, tho once I'd finished, I was almost gagging and had the meat sweats 🍖 . We then retreated to the comfy chairs by the jungle pool, the ones that look like they're made from Cadbury chocolate fingers (which by the way, are crap now, nowt like they used to be). Just before sunset 📷 I again set up my camera to do a time-lapse, and beat my son (at last) at table tennis 🏓 ... wife and I, along with mother and Stepdad turned in about 11.30, and left son to it. He eventually rolled in at 3.30 am, with a story to tell !! He'd made some mates and was shooting hoops when some " absolutely smashed out his face " rich guy from the yacht club comes into the sports hall , he bets my son he can't score a basket first time, £50 .... son makes the shot :-) geezer, honourably hands over a nice fresh £50 note :-) then calls over a waiter, wanting to buy everyone shots ● thankfully the bar was closed. Son was buzzing lol.

If " drunk rich guy " happens to be reading this, I'll be in the sports hall shooting hoops until 2am :-) I'll happily take your ££££ ;-)

Butter Watch

Breakfast :- Dwayne " the rock " Johnson

Lunch :- Julian Clary

Dinner :- Grant Mitchell

Day 4...

Up and at it fairly early today as we are getting off the ship :-) and happy to be joined at breakfast by my beloved, with son in the room with us, she's getting plenty of beauty sleep, doesn't even need to use the " not tonight, I've a headache " excuse :-) . Was nice for me, I didn't have to do the " it's a knockout " routine back to the room, no spilt juice or dropped Crossiants (I always wipe them on my trousers before giving them to her)

Son didn't wanna come today, so we left him to his slumber after him rolling in at 3.30am, also makes for a cheaper trip out, he always (conveniently) leaves his wallet at home on any shopping trips, much like his siblings ●

So brekky done, the 2 of us made our way off the ship :-) . We didn't bother with a shuttle bus, we opted to walk, burn of some of the thousands of calories we've consumed over the last 3 day's. We headed along off towards the beach, lovely to hear the waves lapping the shore, see the golden, well kept sand, and, very much a highlight for me, BOOBS :-), lots of em lol, I now realise why I love Spanish beaches lol 🌑 (I believe objectifying is fine on holiday 🌑) . We then took a walk around the harbour and a couple of shop's, getting ourselves a nice ice-cream each and the Obligatory fridge magnet 🧲, if we continue cruising 🚢 we'll need a bigger fridge!!! Clocked up an impressive 11000 steps, and only spent €30 🌑.

Back in time for a late lunch, so went again to the buffet and found the Son with his Nan and Grandad filling up on pizzas, hotdogs and Redbull, no wonder he's not rolling in until the early hours 🌑, can't believe how much he can put away 🌑, very much his father's son

After lunch I went back to the room for a shower, I was smelling like an empty pringles tube (the sour cream n chives) after the walk, and wanted to slap some sudacrem on my chub rub, unfortunately couldn't find it, so used a sachet of mayo from the buffet, (I've been stockpiling them along with the salt, pepper, ketchup etc to stash in the glove box of my van when home 🌑 brought an extra rucksack to assist.).

Once showered and mayoed I went and found wonder woman, she was sunbathing towards the back of the boat with me mother and ol fella, son off making the most of being able to use his phone whilst docked. I got us all some cold drinks, but wound the wife up when I placed the cold coke can on her bum cheek, I'll not repeat what she called me, but it sounded like what the boat drops in the water when docked ..... After about an hour, in what felt like an oven, our son appeared, needing me to sign a waiver for the water slides. I decided to join him, as unfortunately for me, the mayo, although soothing on chub rub, starts to stink after baking in the sun, and attracts flys 🦋 so the water slides would be a fun way to spend the remainder of the afternoon, and would be a good alternative to the shower, genius ⚫ ... and what fun it was, tho getting out the tubes you sit in was not an easy task I'll tell ya. Went to the buffet again for evening dinner, again a great selection to be had, tho I haven't seen many obvious vegan options (I have a vegan back home, so it's a habit that I look now) thankfully I'm full on carnivorous. Dinner was made even better by the appearance of dolphins 🐬, the sea was really calm, so loads came out to play, maybe it was the calamari (I thought was pasta) that I lobbed overboard enticing them in ⚫

We finished the evening of in the downstairs bar, listening to the pianist and violinist play, most relaxing, i also went to future cruises to price up a Caribbean cruise 🛳 on Seascape ⚫, I can finally use the Jack Sparrow hat I bought at Disney World again ⚫ tho I won't be booking onboard, think my travel agent will get a better price ⚫

BUTTER WATCH..
Those new to my blogs, I rate the butter on a hardness scale, but use celebrities as my gauge instead of numbers :-)
Those jumping in at blog 2/3 should

A. give yourselves a slap for missing out
B. get back and read them all :-)

Breakfast :- Steven Segal
Lunch :- Ant and Dec
Dinner :- Conor McGregor

Disclaimer :-
Mayonnaise is in no way a good substitute for
Sudacrem .

Request :- anyone have an ice pack, I may require one
when my beloved reads the BOOB bit ●

No blog tomorrow, its a sea day and I ain't forking out for
WiFi, not made of money :-)
So I'll double up when we hit Le Harve ●

Day 5..
My first offering today is an apology, apparently a few
snowflakes have taken offence at my " boring/not funny
" post's. Well there's not enough snowflakes to enable
me to make my very own Olaf, so they can bypass my
post's or just " Let It Go " ●
Didn't have breakfast today, managed a lie in for a
change, a very rare occurrence back on dry land, so
most welcome.
Our port of call today was La Coruna, again, just wife
and myself making it ashore, and quite glad we did, I'd

wanted to go here and show the wife the statue I'd modeled for at a still life class a few years ago, I'm guessing they ran out of bronze tho, as a few inches were definitely missing, my nose is much bigger ●
We spent a few hours meandering around the harbour and got some cracking pics of the ship ⛴ and bought another 75 fridge magnets and 36 keyring's to share amongst our 5 friends back home. Had some fun teasing the many fish in the harbour, kicking the discarded fag end's that littered the pathway into the water, watching them going crazy thinking it was food :-), I'll properly feed them later though, I've at least 5 crossiants and a couple pain o chocolates I can lob off the balcony, they'll think it's Christmas 🎄.
Back on board, we had more of an afternoon snack than full on lunch, I've noticed the buttons on my trousers are almost at bursting point, and I've not had an Eartha Kitt for 3 day's, not that I can't, just scared of another injury to the gooch when wiping (day one slip) and the lack of a nail brush, the one ply bog roll that's supplied just don't cut the mustard (marmite :-)) !!! Bringing my own cushelle/andrex next trip ●
The sun came out again for the afternoon, so had a little dip and a sunbathe, amazingly I've not burnt yet, I normally get caught out and end up looking Deadpool !!
Evening was again spent at the buffet, absolutely nothing against the main restaurant, we just, at this moment, prefer the freedom the buffet has to offer. It's very much like " kid in a sweet shop " for a porker like me ● and and the pizza is absolutely phenomenal, I'm gonna miss it when we have to leave ●

The evening was spent down at the infinity bar, it's a very good place to people watch, and amazingly I spotted a cracking fella that runs a local shop back home, what are the chances!!! Wife and I said a quick hello, then left him to it, after all, he's made his escape from everyday hustle and bustle of Birmingham life and its abundance of roadmen, don't wanna spoil his holiday by him knowing our roadman is with us ●

Watched a great 3 piece band, all the way from Brazil play on the small stage down there, they were absolutely fantastic, very easy listening, the lead vocalist was absolutely gorgeous (looked like Veronica from Riverdale) and had a lovely soothing voice, her rendition of Ed Sheerans " ripped jeans " was sublime. Highlight tonight was getting recognised and told my blogs were ace, even asked for my autograph :-) ●

Retreated to bed around midnight, took myself onto the balcony first to administer some of the cream the wife bought from the spa onto my wipe injury, very difficult to reach, but managed in the end with a mascara brush, chose the " Max Factor " , couldn't bring myself to use the " Jeffry Star " round the back :-) . Now soothed I turned in for the night and was out like a light, the beds are super comfy.

Butter Watch

Breakfast :- N/A
Lunch :- Tom Cruise
Dinner :- Jackie Chan

Day 6

Sea day today and didn't start brilliantly, wife couldn't find her mascara brush and wasn't happy that her new cream was two thirds gone ● my gooch however is not only healed, it's now looking 10 years younger. Unfortunately I'm likely to be walking with a limp when my beloved finally catches up on these blogs ●

Back on the brekky today and was accompanied by the wife and son, tho once at the buffet he hooked up with his new found pals, MSC's very own Roadman crew, all donned out in Crocs (very trendy apparently) and Boss/Hilfiger/Off White shorts and t-shirt combo, all the best AAA+ local market/Facebook marketplace buys 👍. We don't see him for the rest of the day, not complaining ●.

Next on the agenda was shopping for a bag for wifey. Well imagine the car boot butcher who sells meat out the back of his lorry meets the Battle of Culloden, and that's what it was like. I got a great spectators view from the ice-cream bar opposite, had a lovely white chocolate waffle cone filled with Nutella and chocolate swirl flavours. Wife managed to grab herself 2x Valentino bags, with matching purse, only suffering 2 broken nails, and one of her hair extensions pulled out, so did very well, unfortunately my pocket didn't, she'll be moaning when we can't afford another cruise next month :-)

But happy her makes my life a much simpler one ●

Whilst battle was in full swing, I was approached by a senior member of the ships staff, who asked " are you Mr Brady ? " " O no " I thought... either the son and his crew have got hammered and caused mayhem or I've been rumbled feeding the dolphin's from the balcony with yesterday's left over French toast and strawberry daiquiri. It was neither. He has seen my blogs and is loving them :-) and looks forward each day to catching up :-)

So, when you see this one, feel free to drop me an inbox with a free upgrade to the yacht club on the cruise we got booked next year ● it will be most gratefully received ●

It was then a quick trip back to the cabin to drop off the purchased bags, and for superwoman to re-attach her hair and wipe the blood from her knuckles before heading to lunch. Buffet again. One of the stations had a fantastic spread of seafood, octopus, squid, prawns..... one of the staff was carrying out a rather large tray of shellfish, I asked " have you got mussels " , he quickly replied " yes " so I said " carry 2 trays then " ●

Afternoon was spent out on the back deck of the ship, we (wife) managed to finally bag one of the comfy wicker beds, likely she was recognised from the ' Battle of The Bag's ' so folk were happy to give one up. Quite a pleasant place to be, and not lava hot today, the French toast and daiquiri obviously worked as I spotted a few more dolphins ●

Quick shower and a re-application of her special cream (ill be entering rear of the year with the miracles it's performing) and it was off for dinner. Suffering heartburn tonight, so I went pretty easy, opting for sweet and sour pork with rice and a side of fish fingers (as you do) . Skipped pudding.

Spent the night down at the infinity bar again, sipping cocktails and watching the same band as last night, Trio La Brava, they were fantastic, and the lead singer, wow, absolutely drop dead gorgeous ⚫ even the wife agreed.

Butter Watch
Breakfast :- Tyson Fury
Lunch :- Anthony Joshua
Dinner :- Deontay Wilder.......
A real heavyweight all day, I've sussed why..... they are surrounding it in ice !!!

Day 7..
Almost home time ⚫
Breakfast today was a liquid one, I had 16 jagerbombs and 1 hard boiled egg, all for good reason..... checked the onboard spend when I woke up !!! Nearly threw myself overboard, but remembered I've got a pack of pork scratchings in the glove box of the car at the port. The beloved son had a ball in the arcade last night, running up a bill of just over £400 !!! Yes, £400!!!! Through the week he'd loaded his own card with cash, no issues, his money. What he didn't realise, neither did I, was he was linked to my card, linked to my bank ⚫ he just continued playing and winning tickets!!!! (I'll add in here, he has autism, so didn't really get it).... anyway, lots of back and forth, between the main reception and the arcade reception, looks like 50% is getting refunded, the rest will be worked off with me next week. Think

MSC need to be a little more clear with how the whole card linked to debit/credit card works. Any future cruises I take, I'll load cash on.

We had planned on getting off in Le Harve, but I, neither wife were in the right frame of mind too, we were both bickering with each other over the previous night. No biggie really, already aired my views on the French (love Christoph Dugarry and Coq au Vin tho) ... ● So it was hot tub time, the wrap around the deck one :-) fabulous and just the relaxing soak I needed. Got out and used the shower by the swimming pool, much to the horror of those sunbathing, forgot it wasn't the room shower, gave everyone a good eyeful, one lady did comment on how youthful my bum looked tho, told her all about the cream ●.

Lunchtime arrived and we all gathered together for a last lunch together, and having only had a liquid breakfast, I more than made up for it, loading my plate like my life depended on it :-) some lovely food again, including spare ribs, tho I think the cows they came from must have been on one of them trendy diets, hopefully I'll find out, and do the same one, they were basically bones :-) Well and truly stuffed we let son go off with his ' massive " :- a few girls part of the crew now (he'd better behave, don't want any angry Dad's banging the door down ●) It was then time to pack the cases. Not something I'm particularly fond of, so I faked a headache (wife's done it all week, apart from the night she was washing her hair) and told her I needed a lie down, taking 2 m and m's to make it look convincing :-) making a miraculous recovery when all was complete, it was BAFTA worthy I tell you :-)

Fortunately, after the packing, there was enough time to catch the last of the afternoon sun, we again managed to bag one of the comfy beds and chilled for a few hours, even got me a cuddle, a kiss and a thank you (verbal kind ●) for the wonderful holiday ●

Evening dinner was a final foray around the buffet, and I went armed with my go-pro, so apologies to those whom I poked the camera in front of, especially sorry to the guy who's soup I dipped it into ● was nice tho, I hadn't got a tissue, so licked it clean ●. I hope you'll all appreciate the pics and videos I share when I'm home :-)

To end the day we headed to the Sky Lounge, adult only bar, and had some final cocktails, whilst watching a fantastic sunset. We then popped down to the main galleria and partook (only for 15 minutes) in the space disco, absolutely awesome, especially the ceiling light show ●

Back up to the room by 11.15 so I can put the cases out ready and get an early night seeing as we have to vacate the room by 7.30 am !!!! Do pop back up to the buffet for a few last slices of pizza. I'm currently stuffing them down along with a rather large bag of peanut m and m's, hopefully wife's asleep or she'll think I'm taking an overdose ● Son's already 15 minutes late back, guessing he's saying his goodbyes.

Butter Watch
Breakfast :- N/A (smashed)

Lunch :- Hagrid
Dinner :- Louis Spence

Not yet farewell from me, I shall finish my blog tomorrow. Even then it won't be goodbye, if you'll have me, I'll be happy to hang around 🌑
Day 8...
Time to go 🌑. Up and at it early this morning, like the majority of us. Had pre breakfast in the room before hitting the buffet, 1 slice and 1 crust of last night's pizza and half a meringue washed down with (I think) the dregs of a Miami Vice.
Wife was reluctant to get up, so i woke the Son first, however this proved difficult, lot's of profanity, shouting and general teenage angst. It was enough to get wife from her pit tho, so job done. Room had to be vacant by 7.30. Before leaving the room i sorted out the tip for house keeping (i know tips are included), left him a lovely selection of pre packed teabags, some sachets of coffee and some creamer to accompany them, even left a bottle of water in the fridge :-) we then grabbed what we were carrying off, knocked on for my folks and all made our way to the buffet. By golly it was busy, finding a seat was like finding Wally. My attempt to get some sausage was like the scene in " The Lion King " where Simba gets caught up in the stampede. Thankfully, I didn't require " Mufasa " I clocked a dropped sausage on the floor, and managed to scoop it up like a fly half 🌑, wife was very grateful of it, she hadn't had a sausage all week 🌑. I waited a few extra minutes to get mine, just enough time to let the stampede settle down :-) .... as

the drinks package was still active, ordered 12 cans of Redbull, 12 Fantas and 16 each of Sprite and Coke to see us through the journey home and for my packed lunch when back at it next week, grabbed some cobs and butter too 🍩

Breakfast done we made our way down to our departure point, had a final hot chocolate and then made our way off the ship. Once through the 2 miles of zig zag gangways, our luggage was already waiting for us, so we made our way out, passing by the ' Nothing to Declare ' desk with ease, just hope the 5000 cigarettes and 60 litres of spirits fit in the boot, don't wanna have to ditch the 12 towels and 2 pillows we acquired :-)

Before we got to our car, we helped my folks get loaded into their car, they have further to drive, so we made sure they were sorted, I even gave them a can of sprite each, will save them stopping at the services, thus saving them a small fortune.

We then proceed to find our car, an easy task, I spray painted in florescent yellow the roofs of the car's either side of it 🍩

Car located, i set about getting loaded and on our way, but before packing the cases in I got out my high viz jacket and trousers, doing my best AA guy impression, made all the more realistic due to the fact a guy behind needed their assistance with a flat battery. I then syphoned out the diesel from the car next to the AA van without raising suspicion and filled mine up. Quickly loaded the car and bolted out of the port for the homeward journey.

On route home, we decided to stop off at Bicester Village. We had saved a few quid on fuel, so thought it a good stop off to pick up myself some New Balance gear for the fitness regime i'm gonna do to shift the cruise pounds I've gained, got to look the part running around the council estate we call home, and a special gift for our Niece who turns 18 this weekend. She's very much a fan of Vivien Westwood, so knowing there was a shop there i popped in, explained my son was feeling sick outside in the car, could they spare a bag I could use to catch any accident he may have travelling home, they duly obliged with one of them nice fancy paper ones with ribbon handles. Left there, and stopped off quickly at the retail park we called at on the journey to the cruise, nipped into the primark for few bits of costume jewellery, took the £1 price stickers off them (got a fivers worth) and put them into the Vivien Westwood bag ⚫ ill be super uncle tomorrow when I see her. Another 90 minutes driving and we make it home. No greeting party waiting for us, just the son's roadman friends who tracked his every move on Snapchat. We were however greeted by the dogs (x 3) who miss us if we go to the toilet, so a week away from them and they loose it, and their ability to control their bladder!!!! I was off course happy to see them, that was until I went out into the back garden!!! It would appear the 2 adult daughters that we left behind are beyond clearing up the mountain of bovril bullets they deposited on my decking !!! Bloody dogs !!! Bloody kids !!!! They also don't know how cook and clean, or get rid of take away boxes, the just eat driver must have had a season ticket to mine this week !!! Wife was fuming 😡 so I retreated to the living room just in time for the F1 qualifying, leaving her to sort out the bomb site. No idea who made poll, I dozed off, only to be selfishly woken up by the sound of the the wife jetwashing the decking down, looked like the Blackpool Pleasure Beach log flume, as she washed the lawn sausages into next doors garden 😅.... Fair play to her, she'd cleaned everywhere, so the good husband I am, I got the daughter to make her a cuppa as a thanks and as an apology for not watering the cress and tomato plants 😂 As great as my nap was, I was still tired, as was the wife from all her hard work, so we retired to bed, accompanied by the dogs, tho only 2 of them thankfully, as eldest daughter sneaked in whilst the decking was getting de pooed, took her dog and made off to her boyfriend's before feeling mom's wrath 😡. Hopefully tomorrow will see the calm after the storm, she's always emotionally charged after the end of a holiday, the unfortunate " back to reality "

Butter Watch
Breakfast :- Ken Barlow
Lunch :- N/A
Dinner :-- N/A we're home and use marg

So that's it, blogs completed.....
Keep watching this space tho, I'll be back very soon with a full review and hints and tips guide 😉

Loved my time sharing with you, loved my time on the ship... back to the day job

Much love Mark..... Helena and Niall...

Dear Mario, Salvatore & Claudia
I hope I find you well ?
My name is Mark, and I write these words to you as a
thank you and as a review of mine, and my families
recent trip on the magnificent Virtuosa, what an
impressive thing she is (gender assuming) !!! I know us
men tend to exaggerate size, but she's huge,
gargantuan in fact. This was a third cruise for myself
and my wife, we were in tow with our youngest child, a
usually grumpy 17 year old son, and my folk's, they in
one cabin, the 3 of us in another. It was however our
first MSC cruise, we previously sailed on P&O Ventura,
Pam and Oswald being excellent hosts, so we did have
a comparison, many area's to gauge you on. You, by a
country mile, win round one, the size comparison,
impressive in both length and girth ●, you definitely
own the bragging rights here. So from the offset, we are
impressed.
The boarding process was seamless, very efficient in
what I guess are still challenging time's for you as a
company, your staff and for us passengers. Yes, there
were lot's of pre departure shenanigans to do, including
still having to stick cotton buds up our nose, (hoping
this will soon become a thing of the past, don't think it's
leaving any time soon, just got to live with it), and
reams of paperwork (went through countless ink
cartridges, and cleaned out my local ryman branch of A4

paper) .... But onboard in 20 minutes, much better than the current goings on at the airports.

Once we got onboard we were left gobsmacked!!! She's just stunning, it's wow after wow after wow. The last time my jaw dropped at such beauty on a boat was when Erica Eleniak made her birthday cake appearance in " Under Seige " :-)

So another round to Virtuosa. The Galleria is beyond incredible, still can't get my breath at the ceiling, a modern day masterpiece, a 21st century Sistine Chapel that is as genius as Michelangelo's artistry, in fact it's better, he likely had the help of the other mutant turtles :-). Then there's the Swarovski stairs, like an Alaskan glacier, the Lady Ga Ga of staircases.

What was needed at this point was to find our room to offload our carry on so as to further explore. We had a balcony room close to the front of the ship that more than met our needs. Plenty room for storage, a lovely bathroom and super comfy beds. Nice that there's a proper size TV too. All immaculately clean. Not that you'll spend much time in here, it really is just a base to sleep and get washed and dressed.

On any holiday, be it a land based hotel or a cruise ship, it's important to get your barings as quickly as possible. This ship again takes the winners crown. Its fully interactive, with touch screens everywhere that will always point you to where you need to be, and an amazingly efficient lift system. Maybe Noah would struggle, it's a bit ahead of the arc, but everyone else, even those oldies who are technophobes should be fine, it's pretty easy. The only real thing to remember is if you need to turn left or right out of the lift to get back to your room :-) it's a long walk of shame if u get it wrong, but excellent for burning calories.

The single most important thing on holiday will no doubt be your drinking and dining experience. Spoilt for choice here. Our first 2 nights, we opted for the included dining restaurant, with a dining time of 6pm. This was where we found one of our first, and pretty much only negative. Firstly, we were assigned a table that was down some steps, we had a wheelchair user with us, so not ideal. The first solution they offered was to carry the wheelchair down, but not really a good solution, I could just see a " Carry On " moment happening, so we politely declined. They then made the decision to move us tables, much the better option. The service in here was great, the food good, but not enough options and felt rushed. Definitely room for improvement here, and not as good as P&O. That said, there are more class options on MSC. I'd be pretty confident that if we were Yacht Club diner's, the experience would have been far better, and no doubt trumped P&O again, maybe one day I'll be affording of the privilege, or bag me a free upgrade ● my inbox is always open to any kind offers, and will always be gratefully received.

So after the first 2 nights, our dining was spent at the buffet. The choice here was always fantastic, and none of us would go hungry, in fact, quite the opposite ● pretty much every sitting I felt like I was fit to burst. The pizza was always to much of a temptation, it would taunt me every time I went by, always unable to resist, moth to a light bulb :-)

We never tried any of the speciality restaurants, didn't feel the need, and didn't really feel it warranted it's price, having checked out a few of the menus.

The drinking at wherever you ended up was most excellent tho. We were on a premium extra package so there was very little that was out of reach, the choices were endless with some fantastic cocktails. Son loved that the Redbull was included in his under 18 package, kept him partying until 4am most nights, can't say we enjoyed the comedown each morning tho, was like an angry bear. Our favourite places to drink were the Skybar and infinity bar. We did check out the robot in the Starship Club, but again, felt it over priced so didn't have a cocktail here, if it was R2D2 or CP30 that made and served me, then maybe I'd have gone for it :-) very cool though, and I'll happily accept any freebies you may want to send me :-)

I do have a future cruise booked on the sister ship Grandiosa ●

Entertaining your guests is something that you're clearly passionate about. There's something for all ages to do or see. We loved the pools, the hot tubs and the parties, the themed nights were fantastically entertaining, and were enjoyed by all. The choice of onboard entertainers was ace, all of the acts/bands we got to see were great. My personal favourite Trio La Brava, loved them.

The staff you employ are first class, nothing is beyond them, and their willingness to provide 100% all the time is to be applauded.

Another win over P&O is the catering to the young on board, those under 18. My son has stated that this has been the best holiday he's ever been on, considering we've taken him and our other children to Walt Disney World a few times, it's a bold statement and kudos to what MSC deliver. The aquapark, sport's hall, the various kids clubs, all brilliant. Then there's the arcade. Here is where I had the biggest issue onboard. My son managed to run up a £400 spend in one evening, in fact, it was pretty much within an hour. We didn't realise his card was linked to my onboard account, as a minor, I assumed it was restricted. Unfortunately this is not the case, you have to request it to have a block on it. I feel that more clarity is required here, I think the block on under 18's should be mandatory, that a request should be made to unblock it, put a max on it, very easy to do I'd think with how the whole system works. That said, I again have to applaud MSC and the staff, they were understanding to what had happened, I'd added that my son has autism, they listened and offered a 50% refund, which I couldn't really argue with, obviously 100% would have been great, but is what is. Luckily for my son, I didn't throw him overboard, close, but he's bigger than me these days lol.

Shopping on board was excellent, some great deals in the duty free, wife got some lovely new handbags that were on special sale, unfortunately the Omega watches were still beyond me, again, I'll happily take a voucher for one, there was a particular Seamaster I had my eyes on :-)

We only booked the holiday 4 weeks prior to sailing, we got it at a great price, and wanted to " test the water's " as we are booked onto Grandiosa to sail the Norwegian

Fjords in August 2023. I'm very glad we did. It delivered everything and more than we could have ever wanted, all boxes ticked, leaving us all very happy, recharged and buzzing for the next one. I'm pretty confident that we'll be onboard again before summer 23, we have well and truly got the cruise bug, and have ABSOLUTELY fallen in love with MSC and look forward to exploring it's fleet :-) currently looking at Seascape, happy to be a test cruiser if required :-)

This post I hope will reach MSC, I'm aware that most of the groups I post in are not officially operated by them. I'd also love them to see my blogs from my time aboard :-)
To those who followed and commented on my blogs, I'm most grateful and I'll be hanging around. I'm looking at blogging on a regular basis and I'm seriously looking at making a book of the Virtuosa blog :-)

Once again, thank you all, love to you all, and happy sailing, I look forward to seeing you onboard in the future.....
Love Mark and the Brady Bunch :-)

Day one after Virtuosa. . ....

Boo :-)

I'm back :-)

Couldn't leave you all could I ●

Sunday for my first offering. Very much the " god I'm home " kinda day. Neither myself or the wife wanted to get out of bed, it's not quite the same, we long to open the curtains to the ocean view's we so loved last week, instead I open them to see a dragon !!! Rub my eyes, look again, still a dragon, and it appears to be angry ●... put my glasses on, still an angry dragon 🐉. Obviously, curious and not really buying it, wife gets up to look and confirms it. It's the woman next door, sat vaping in her T.Rex onsie !!! Thought I'd woken up in Jurassic Park. Up now, and decide on the buffet. Then remember, no buffet, we're back home ●. Then remember there's no milk. No cereal or bread either!!! So off to Asda I go. Not something I am fond of at the best of times, really detest it on Sunday, seems everyone is out and decending upon the supermarket!! I try and make it a quick in and out. Got the milk without incident, couple of other bits n bobs without issue. Bread isle a different story, u see it's placed right next to the bargain bin!! Pandemonium would be my description, folk going mad for over reduced ham, snack eggs and a few packs of them pro biotic yogurt drinks, like Tramps on chips they were !!! Anyway, I pushed on through, grabbed me a Warburtons (extra thick) and headed to the checkout, only just managing to bypass the " mate who I ain't seen in ages, who you know will keep you chatting forever " .... lucky escape. Chose the self checkout, bad choice, they never work !! Half hour later I make it back to the car. Get the aircon going and chill for a few minutes to eat my snack eggs and drink the yogurt drinks, tho 11 in one go was not my finest moment, at least I'm back where I can use Andrex ●

Once home I went and " dropped the kids at the pool ", took a double flush, got carried away with the Andrex :-) and then accosted the sky remote and the comfy chair and puffè in readiness for the F1 ●. Got the wife to sort me a nice glass of squash and Pot Noodle (green one) and kicked back. What a great race it was :-) Very thankful the halo did it's job, big crash that was!!! The drawback to the delay in the race was the " how much longer is it on for " nags I was getting!!! We had to go to see our Niece, her 18th :-). So at the drop of the chequered flag I sent them out to wait in the car, told them I'd be minutes, half hour later, didn't wanna miss the podium or the recap, I joined them. Wife seemed annoyed, I guess she's still missing the ship :-)

Anyway, we arrived at my Bro's (he's technically not my bro, just my bestie). What a nightmare to park first off !!! Think everyone who'd been at Asda were in his street, so I parked on the grass, making sure to park as close to the " don't park on the grass " sign :- if it's not seen, who can complain ●. Tapping on the window to gain attention, and pulling faces behind his head, as u do (he had his back to the window) I realised that it was a balloon, not his bald noggin !!! ●

Once in, we battled through the sea of shoes, you have to take them off, they still at that " u can't wear shoes on the new carpet " stage. Niece was obviously delighted to see us, and was buzzing when she saw the Vivien Westwood bag I had ●

She loved what was inside too (beautiful bracelet) 🔴 as if I'd really give her Primark stuff , I've put them away for our wedding anniversary 💜 wife will love em. Got me and wife the biggest slice of birthday cake, which was bloody lovely, very messy tho, dropped huge chunk of the sticky icing and a blob of jam on the carpet, quickly picked it up and dropped it down the back of the sofa, and rubbed the rest into the carpet with whoever left the cardigan on the back of the sofa :-) . Told them all about the holiday, and hopefully they'll join us cruising soon :-) . Getting tired, and knowing it was the dreaded ' back to work day ' in the morning we called it a day 🔴 Upon leaving could hear some expletives, one of the younger kids there had apparently wedged cake down the back of the sofa and got jam on the carpet 🔴 Result :-) .. . .

Butter Watch is unfortunately not applicable, it shall return for my next cruise though 🔴

Still penning my hints and tips, probably do it tomorrow when I'm meant to be back grafting 🔴

Enjoy xx love to all x

Day 2 off Virtuosa…

Today marked the inevitable. The dreaded back to work. Really couldn't be doing with it, so I phone up the boss to say I wasn't coming. Went to answer phone, always a relief, so I left a message, putting on my best " I'm dying

" voice, always best to try and be convincing, said i must have picked up a bug from the boat. No sooner had I done that, my phone pinged, I'd an answer message. Imagine my surprise when the playback was the Oscar worthy speech I'd just left. Forgot I'm my own boss ● Unfortunately, that comes with responsibility, so I had to drag myself out of bed and get back at it, got a cruise (or many) to pay for. Tried not to disturb the wife, unfortunately the dogs had other ideas ●, obviously my fault for letting them into the room lol ●. To make ammends , and now we had milk in the house I did her breakfast in bed, lovingly preparing a cup of tea and a bowl of coco pops (well the cheap aldi version of) . Before I deprted I also had to feed the dogs. Not having much time due to having to do wifes breakfast they had to settle for scrambled eggs (a poached for the corgi), bacon (fat removed),sausage, black pudding and lambs liver, served with warm milk. Daughter smelt the bacon cooking so also wanted breakfast, so I duly obliged, chucked her up a packet of smokey bacon crisps ● she couldn't really moan, she wanted a lift to work. Hurried her along before the other's woke up, they'd have all started wanting feeding !!! Made it out the house at 8.30, with Daughter in tow, tho now moaning because we're " going in the van " !!! Apparently not the best of looks for a newly promoted lettings consultant!! Well sorry it's not an Audi ! She then had a hissy fit en route, cursing at the lollipop lady for allowing kid's to cross when she's in a rush, and for the bus in front daring to stop to let folk on and off, She'll be on it tomorrow !!! Thankfully we made it on time, tho she'll be brewing come dinner time, left her packed lunch, I noticed as she was getting out, but clocked the dairylea dunkers that were part of it, and knew I'd be peckish during the day 🌑

So onwards to work. Thankfully, on arrival to my workshop, there was nothing unexpected waiting for me, no unwelcome bills, and no new deliveries, so I could ease myself back into it fairly gently. Made my Monday morning calls to those I do work for to let em know I was back, and picked a few easy jobs to do, not that any of what I do is easy. Job no.1 was a fair drive away, so had my breakfast on the way, pickled onion space raiders with half a litre of R White's, pretty flat having been perched on the dashboard since before my jollies. For the most, I work on my ones, so always great to see pals in the trade. Today, after arriving at my first " port of call " (not the same ring to it when away from the ship) I spotted my pal before he had clocked me, so not one to miss an opportunity, I crept up on him and bellowed like a bear!!! Absolutely bricked it he did, fell to the floor I got him that good 🌑. As I turned around, laughing until I cried, a familiar face was stood watching and literally wetting himself. This was in fact my pal, the guy who was now (thankfully) up from the floor was his new colleague, whom I'd not met before :-) quite the introduction I think 🌑, good job I hadn't done the old " shorts down " job on him lol. Unfortunately for him, it probably won't be the last time I get him, I can't help myself, kind of a habit amongst us all in the trade, if one of us spots the other first without them seeing. Early winter morning's are the worst/best especially as my/our job is undertaken in cemeteries and churchyards, you're often on edge. Anyway, after having my fun and telling my pal all about the cruise (him and his family are joining us next year on the Fjords cruise) I left him and his now recovered pal too it so I could crack on with my job 🌑. Got it completed pretty quickly, I'd already done most of it before my holiday, just adding the main part back, a nice restoration job. Sent pics to the customer, who responded almost instantly, was thrilled and forwarded payment on too 🌑 always a bonus. Couple more different cemeteries to visit, couple of quotes to get through and I was done, nice early finish. Obviously didn't want wife to know I was done early, so went and parked up for a few hours, jumped into the back of the van and had a kip :-). Woke about 5, rang ahead to get the wife to run me a bath and make me some super noodles, as I was starving, (the dairylea dunkers didn't fair well sat on the dash in the direct sunlight, the sticks were OK, but the cheese tasted like a vegans fart) . Got in, and good as gold, my bath was already done, and I could smell the noodles cooking. Went upstairs, stripped off and jumped straight into the bath 🛁. Jumped straight back out again, cussing and cursing, it was bloody freezing. It was then she called up telling me my noodles were done, and she'd run me my bath whilst I ate them. Bloody daughter had a bath last night and hadn't pulled the plug out !!! Why can't they do simple things? 🌑

So went down stairs to get my noodles. This didn't go well either. Having jumped in and then out the bath, knowing I'd soon be back in it, I went downstairs as was, as naked as the day I was born. Didn't know wife's friends were round, never been so embarrassed, the water, as I said, was freezing ●, I'm what's referred to as a ' grower ' ●. I make a hasty retreat, grabbing noodles on the way past the kitchen and go run the bath myself. Unfortunately, they're now cold, but I eat them anyway ●. Get myself into the bath and finally chill, tho do hear the wife's friends having a giggle as they leave, sure it was at my expense, heard one of them mention an acorn and another Warwick Davis !!!! Don't like her friends anyway......

Bath done, I decided bed was the best option, unfortunately couldn't get to sleep straightaway, probably down to the van nap ● so started sorting through my pics from the cruise and starting my hints and tips, I'll be sharing soon x

As for blogging, I'm thinking a weekly blog if folk wanna continue to hear my ramblings, and daily ones when on my jollies :-)
Maybe one day a book 📖

See u soon x Mark.

One week off Virtuosa....

Hi cruisers, I hope I find you all well ●
If you're reading this, you've made it, you survived the first week back ● all being well, without incident (2 ply certainly helps) ...

So you'll have read (you'd better have) my first 2 blogs after returning, this is those day's after, a weekly one seems more the ticket :-)

Speeding ticket!!! Mail arrived on Tuesday with a lovely gift for me !!! The week before I'd taken my beloved youngest daughter and her pal to see Billie Eilish. Because I'm Superdad (Super everything I'll let u know) I dropped her friend home after the gig, all the way to Burton from Brum. What a nightmare journey !!! Apparently, roadworks are better done at night, so there were roads closed everywhere. Eventually got her home, but got flashed on the way back, down a dark and winding country lane, middle of nowhere at 1am !!! 36 in a 30 !!! I mean come on !!! Gimme a break!! I'm a Peugeot driver now, ditched the Beemer, was to fast, and now u catch me .... £100 fine and 3 points or the option of a speed awareness course. Think I'm gonna take the corse, should provide me a good day's blogging :-)

Wednesday brought about the wonder that is IKEA. Apparently we need 3 x new gleftgs, 1 x yunbek, a selection of snafburls and a replacement hinge for the kitchen legenhas. The only good that comes of such a trip is the meatballs :-) Wife kindly treated me to 2 plates :-) my reward for going. Before eating them tho, I set about arranging them like a stack of cannon ball's, Lord Nelson would have been most impressed. They went down a treat, love the gravy they're served with, but not a fan of the jam, I mean who has jam with balls and gravy !!! Had the obligatory hotdog too upon leaving, looked like E.T's finger, tasted like a prostate Dr's finger, very disappointed. We left with all we needed, and nothing flat packed to assemble once home thankfully, always like a Krypton Factor challenge them things, and I've always a screw and the odd panel left over.

Thursday and Friday saw me very busy at graft, playing catch up after my jollies, unfortunately no magic fairies did my work. I did however have help, I've got the son helping, paying back the arcade spend lol, can't say he's happy, but got to learn lol. The drawback is the constant moaning " I can't do it dad " or " how much more we got to do ? ". I will, in his defence add it is heavy going, quite often 3/400 kilo job's, hopefully he'll soon be a millionaire YouTuber or TikToker, then I'll retire and he can pay for wife and I to cruise the world ●.

To be fair, the week rolled by, much faster than expected. My weekend plans are to do as little as possible, I'm gonna watch sport, tho not the women's Euros, i just don't get it, I'm sorry, please don't hang me lol, it's just not for me, though im sure any one of the teams would beat my team Birmingham City ● and try to sort my pics and videos out for uploading ● No doubt this will be scuppered by kid's and dog's wanting lifts and walks.

I was tho right, the scuppering began just after bedtime. My lovely wife suffers from restless leg syndrome, or as I like to call it ' kick your wonderful, hard working hubby to death syndrome ' , I'd imagine a night in the octagon would be a more comfortable night. Add to that a needy cockapoo, who decides she needs to drop a bovril bullet just as I'm finally falling off to sleep. So I make my way out of the bedroom and downstairs, no easy feat I'll tell you, as I don't wanna open up my eye's, they've developed that nice sticky crust, and make it unscathed past the minefield of Nike Air Max and Coke cans. Get to the back door and let her go do her business, something that during the day, takes 2 minutes at most, not the night time log dropping tho, that takes forever. Finally, after me threatening her with a foot up the fudge factory, she nonchalantly walks in, and proceeds to drag her arse across the laminate, thankfully just seeing to an itch I'm guessing, as I felt around with my bare foot, no sign of a dropped off clingon 🔵

She legs it back upstairs ahead of me, I again, eye's still closed make my way back up. Before going back to bed I think it a safe bet to go the bog. Now in our house, it's a rule that all toilet functions are taken in the sit down position. So I feel my way into the bathroom, when I make a big mistake!!! I slam myself down on the pan, forgetting, in my still sticky eyed/sleepy state, to lift the seat !!! The scream I let out was akin to the waxing scene in ' 40 Year Old Virgin ' ... obviously this woke the house, wife kicks off the toilet door to find me lying on the floor, cupping and whimpering. Kids enter next, and find the the site of me , lying there like a new born, boxer's round my ankles, wife checking my nads are still in place, hilarious, quickly getting their phones out to Instagram/Snapchat me in my not so finest hour 🔵

Wife calms me down and offers to rub some voltarol in, "no thanks" I reply, she didn't wanna rub anything when I asked earlier on 🔵. The only good to come of the episode was the fact she was now awake, so I could thankfully get to sleep before she started practicing her Ju-jitsu again ●

Woke up, not exactly feeling fresh as a daisy, but after a quick feel, they were both still in the onion bag. The downside, I'm walking like a penguin 🐧 Wife was in a good mood tho, and offered me breakfast in bed, thought it funny to bring me 2 scotch eggs ● and apparently I'll be going viral on TikTok !!! Feeling slightly sorry for me, both wife and kids were happy to leave me be for the rest of the day, so I took my place in the comfy chair, and watched the rugby, the F1 sprint and some of the Tour de France (brutal) . Bedtime soon rolled around, luckily, eldest daughter is at her boyfriend's, so I jump in her bed for a nice and hopefully peaceful night's sleep, but not before blogging my happenings for you guy's :-)

Until the next installment, goodnight, Godbless and sweet dreams ●......

Week 2 off Virtuosa..

Sup folks ● .. hope I find you all well ?

I'm happy to report that after last week's toilet seat episode, I'm almost fully recovered, the penguin walk is now more chav/roadman walk, and I complete this look (so as to blend in) by wearing my son's Hoodrich trakky bottoms and placing my hands inside the front of my boxer's ●

I do however have a bathroom incident to report.

There's 3 x women under the roof of Brady Manor, so

the bathroom is very much like a superdrug store, bottle's everywhere. Yesterday, I take my evening shower, and reach for one of the bottle's, assuming it was shampoo. It smelt lovely, and lathered up just fine. Just as I was to rinse it off, the electric went. Unfortunately no 50p's left on the side, we'd used the last one for the TV. So I got one of the kid's to break open their money box so we could top the meter up, and luckily there was quid in there, bingo :-) Top up successful, the lekky came back on. I did the rinse off quickly, as the water was freezing ● exited the shower and dried and dressed. When pulling on my socks I noticed my hands were green. Now I'm no David Banner, so I quickly realised what I'd done. A quick glance in the mirror confirmed this. My ' George Clooney ' grey look was no more... I'm now sporting the ' Billie Eilish ' look.... I'm the Bad Guy.....duh ●
Hopefully the searing heat that we're enduring will burn it out. Speaking of the heat, it's not been pleasant grafting out in it. It's like I'm made of mozzarella, truly melting and giving off a cheesy smell by the end of the day ● I do seem to be back into the routine of work, definitely missing the eating routine the ship offered tho, it's not the same eating monster munch for breakfast. I did have a Toby carvery after work on Tuesday, but can't go back there now, I forgot I wasn't on the ship, and left without paying ●. Gonna try Morrisons salad bar next week ● Talking of work, had an issue that is one I always worry will happen. Had a call from a customer who couldn't find the memorial I'd installed for their dad. I'd only gone and installed it on the wrong grave ●.

Thankfully they were great about it, turns out it wasn't my fault, the council issue me a permit for each stone, they had made an error with the number. The family actually found it funny, saying their beloved Dad would be laughing too. I'm off to place it upon the correct grave this morning.

Another plus from the week is I've booked a nice little weekend break away, off to my favourite destination, The Scottish Highlands 🌑 to leap from waterfalls, will definitely make for a good blog if I don't kill myself. Wife not coming, she doesn't approve of my lunatic behaviour when im up there, she's gonna stay home with the dog's looking for our next cruise, any recommendations welcome. Myself, the son, my daughter and her girlfriend are going, and hopefully the sun will be still shining. We're hoping to hook up with a friend my son made on the ship, seems there were many from Scotland on board 🌑. Heading for some fun at Falls of Falloch, leaping the fall's 🌑

Sorry this blog is a little drab, I'll definitely make up for it on the next one 🌑

If there was Butter Watch this week, then they'd all be George from Rainbow with the way the sun has been :-)

Peace out and love to all x The Brady Bunch

Tips, do's and don'ts .....

Journey to the port :-

If travelling with wife/children/teenagers wear headphones, that way you'll not have to hear the 100 " we nearly there yets ? "

If travelling with just your wife, make sure she's actually packed you something to wear.

If travelling with just your husband, make sure you've packed him something to wear.

If travelling from Scotland, knock the car out of gear, it's all downhill, you'll save a fortune on fuel.

If travelling by public transport, in particular, train or plane, good luck, there's likely a strike.

If you park your car at the port, remember to remove the half eaten pork pie and half drunken milkshake from the dashboard, not pretty upon your return.

Paint a massive florescent X on the cars either side of yours, that way yours out when on top deck before setting sail.

Before setting sail, when on top deck, having spotted your car, take a pic, it'll come in handy when you can't remember where it is after a week on the pop.

Yes that's your ship, yes it's massive, yes it's a wonder it floats, yes there's enough lifeboats for all.

No it's not going to sink.

Yes it's bigger than Titanic.

Yes, I know Titanic sank, we won't.

Once onboard :-

Take 2 balls of string, run each from your cabin to the bar and the buffet respectively, you'll never go hungry or thirsty.

Don't run in the corridors, it's no fun hitting someone as they exit their cabin.

Play knock door run.

Play lift roulette. Whilst waiting for your lift to arrive, you face the doors, middle finger 🖕 up for when the doors open. Works the same when in the lift.

No crabbing lines are to be used from the balcony.

No naked sunbathing on the balcony, I apologise now to those I scarred for life.

Each morning take 12 towels to the pool, lay each out on various beds, then when your ready to sunbathe after lunch, you'll have the pick of them.

Take a fake poo and some fishing line, attach line to fake poo. Once in hot tub, if someone you don't like the look of tries to enter, float the turd, if someone smoking hot appears, reel it in.

If u have to, fart when in the hot tub, no one will know it's you.

If you've had curry the night before, don't fart in the hot tub, everyone will know it's you.

Men, don't remove your trunks to shower at the poolside showers, I again apologise to those whom I've scarred for life.

Fitties, do remove your bikinis at the poolside showers.

Don't bomb from the top deck into the pool below, it's definitely not deep enough.

Yes you'd kill yourself jumping from the top deck into the sea.

Don't flush the cabin toilet whilst still sitting on it, I've lost my spleen.

Don't attempt love making whilst crossing the Bay of Biscay, accidents can and do happen, my wife is still limping.

Don't go to the toilet whilst crossing the Bay of Biscay, accidents can and do happen, I'm still limping.

If travelling with kids, leave em to it, they can't go anywhere, you go the bar and get smashed.

If travelling without kids, go the bar and get smashed.

Get to the buffet early to avoid the stampede.

Be careful with the butter, it can be very destructive.

For fun and frolics, stick an upside down pineapple outside your room.

To avoid divorce, don't stick an upside down pineapple outside your room.

Whoever you are, wherever you're from, live, love and laugh :-)
Enjoy your cruise and please feel free to add to my tips :-)

My very final tip, and the most important.....
Don't take life (or me) to seriously x
Love and happy cruising to all, I hope to meet many of you onboard one day :-)

OMG !!! I've only been away a few weeks and there's mutiny!!! Well I'm not having it !! This weekend seems to be National Karen Weekend. Never seen so many snowflakes, like a blizzard out there, was thinking about getting my sledge out. What is it with those who think they're entitled; that they should get their ' strawberry daiquiri ' in an instant !!! I bet they wouldn't complain if ' sex on the beach ' took ages, or they got an ' orgasm ' instead ● if I was their barman, the latter would take at least an hour ●

Oooo, there's not enough food for me to eat !!! ARE YOU KIDDING??? There's enough food to feed Gemma Collins on that boat, and more choices of things to eat than Katie Price has had men. All of it cooked well, served hot, and served ALWAYS with a smile. The main restaurant's may not always have something you desire, but the buffet will. Also, if, for example you want breakfast, and breakfast finishes at 10.30, don't rock up at 10.25 and start barking when they haven't what you want left. I'm always at the breakfast buffet for when it opens, I need the sustenance after laying out 50 towels on the front row poolside loungers ●

Too many kids !! Er hello !! It's the summer holidays. Clearly you didn't do your homework ●. And what's wrong with lots of kid's??? Were you not a child yourself?? Remember, these children are our future, teach them well and let them lead the way, show them all the beauty the possess inside. Give them a sense of pride to make it easier. Let the children's laughter remind us how we used to be. ... .. ●

Getting off the boat for excursions .... there's potentially 5k people on the ship, it's not rocket science that its gonna be busy is it !!! Get your arse up out of bed if you want to disembark early enough to enjoy what your destination has to offer, just because you're on holiday, it doesn't mean things should run to your timetable.
And bare in mind there maybe other ships at the same port, doing the same. This is especially important if your port is reached by tender. I'd send you over on a lilo ⬤ or one of them big inflatable flamingos or unicorns, and I'd send you the wrong way, and wave at you as we pass you by out at sea later on ⬤
My cabin ain't big enough !!! What you expecting?? Especially those who opted for inside cabins. Firstly, you know what your booking at the time of booking, there's plenty information given as to the size and layout of the room. U probably, at the time of booking thought " ill book the cheapest and smallest room, then complain about not having enough space and bag me a cheeky free upgrade " Well bad luck.
The entertainment wasn't very good...
Well it is. It may not be to your liking. But the entertainment is first class. Don't rock up expecting a full stadium concert by Ed Sheeran, or Tom Cruise performing in the theatre, if you do, obviously disappointment will follow. I bet some complain they've not got corrie or eastenders on !!!
The biggest bug bare I have is those complaining of rude staff !! Na, I don't believe you one bit. It's more than their job is worth for starters. You come on holiday in

Diva mode, all " I asked for only yellow m&m's and there's a green one in there "...

Leave that attitude on shore with you. It's like you loose all respect for others when on holiday.

The likelihood is if you're on a taster cruise, then you've payed pennies, a week cruise probably less than a grand, anything longer, then a few grand each. What you get is DEFINITELY more than your monies worth on MSC. They aren't Cunard and don't pretend to be. They offer absolutely fantastic value for money, and have brought cruises to to many that maybe only ever dreamt of going on one. All you snooty ' Hyacinth Buckets ' I'd suggest shopping at aldi and lidl for a few months instead of Waitrose and M&S, and with the money you save you can book yourself onto the Cunard you CLEARLY deserve, and enjoy your salmon and cucumber sandwiches and Dom Perignon..... we won't miss you.....

If we pass by each other on the great blue ocean, I'll be the one mooning you from my balcony ●

Footnote....

Cunard don't do pineapples ●

Much love to MSC ●

Some facts about MSC Virtuosa.

All measurements were based on (correct at the time of posting 28.08.22) the average pineapple as supplied by Aldi (other supermarkets are available)

• Weighs in at 181,541 GT or 181 million pineapples 🍍

• Measures 1,087 feet long or 2160 pineapples laid out tip to toe 🍍 🍍

• Stands at 213 feet high or 420 pineapples balanced on top of one another 🍍 🍍 🍍

• Offers 19 decks or 19 pineapples if each deck were a pineapple 🍍

• Carries a maximum guest capacity of 6,334 travelers (though the normal double occupancy is 4,842 passengers) or 504000 pineapples 🍍

• Carries 1,704 crew members atop the total number of guests or 136000 pineapples 🍍

Cost to build £750 million or 750 million pineapples 🍍 from Aldi or 300 million Waitrose pineapples 🍍

No pineapples were injured during the making of this post.....
Footnote :- I don't even like pineapple lol 🌑
Agadoo doo doo, is that a pineapple I see?
Agadoo doo doo, I hope that pineapples for me!

To the left, to the right; no, just put it upside down.
And you will soon discover fun and frolics will be
found....

I met a hula mistress somewhere on MSC
Where she was selling pineapple on a cruise on the sea.
And when I spoke to the girl, she said she'd teach me to
swing
She laughed and whispered to me, yes it's really a
thing!!

Some lovely fun on the sea
For you and for me
When I show you my dong
We'll all be singing this song

Agadoo doo doo, is that a pineapple I see?
Agadoo doo doo, I hope that pineapples for me!
To the left, to the right; no, just put it upside down.
And you will soon discover fun and frolics will be
found....

Agadoo doo doo, is that a pineapple I see?
Agadoo doo doo, I hope that pineapples for me!
To the left, to the right; no, just put it upside down.
And you will soon discover fun and frolics will be
found....
Then down below deck
They gather romance
She showed me much more
What was under her pants

Agadoo doo doo, is that a pineapple I see?
Agadoo doo doo, I hope that pineapples for me!
To the left, to the right; no, just put it upside down.
And you will soon discover fun and frolics will be
found....

Agadoo doo doo, is that a pineapple I see?
Agadoo doo doo, I hope that pineapples for me!
To the left, to the right; no, just put it upside down.
And you will soon discover fun and frolics will be
found....

Some lovely fun on the sea
For you and for me
When I take off my thong
We'll all be singing this song

Agadoo doo doo, is that a pineapple I see?
Agadoo doo doo, I hope that pineapples for me!
To the left, to the right; no, just put it upside down.
And you will soon discover fun and frolics will be
found....
Agadoo doo doo, is that a pineapple I see?
Agadoo doo doo, I hope that pineapples for me!
To the left, to the right; no, just put it upside down.
And you will soon discover fun and frolics will be
found....
Day 1

Gooooooooooooooooooodddd morning MSC...... or afternoon, or if you're really late to the party, good evening...

The blog is back, as is butter watch. This time, tho, butter watch will be more politically correct and feature ladies on the scale of hardness...

So let's get this ship sailing.....

Our embarkation time was 4pm, so as we are 2.5 hours away from Southampton, I had the alarm set for 5am, I'd have made it 4, but was being a little thoughtful with it being a Sunday ● Helena (wifey, thought I'd use our real names this time around) thankfully didn't hear it, she's not exactly a morning person, so I luckily avoided an early morning beating.

Scrap the ' avoided a beating ' bit. Dog's put pay to that!!! Whilst I was lovingly preparing a full breakfast, with all the bells and whistle's, the Dog's managed to get in from the garden, make it up the stairs and proceed to dry themselves on our bed, much to the displeasure of Helena, don't think she appreciated x 3 Dog's dragging their bumholes across her newly highlighted blonde lock's.. ● Didn't help that I'd run out of milk for her weatabix and morning tea, apparently ' last night's McDonald's chocolate milkshake ' isn't a good milk replacementeither!! ●

O well ●... An hour had now passed, and I had completed the 3 s' (S*#t, Shower & Shave) so I went off out the house to load up the car. No easy feat I'll tell you, it was like playing Tetris with all the luggage and can's of Pringles (I'll be selling telescopes and binoculars onboard). Luckily there was just enough room in the boot for my JD carrier bag (bloody 25p each now) that contained my clobber.

Another reason we needed to leave a bit earlier was I needed to pick up my new glasses on the way. Couldn't believe the price of them when I got there tho !!! £2 !!! Why they call it poundland nowadays is beyond me !!! They even have some items that are a fiver !!! Seems like they too are taking advantage of these price hikes !!! Dread to think how much a Freddo Frog is in these times of hardship. Anyway, I got myself 2 pair's, I could justify it because I managed to save myself a small fortune by getting a fake Toblerone for a quid, instead of getting one on the ship that would have required a mortgage.

Detour done and we were finally on our way 🙌. The good thing with it being a Sunday was less traffic on the roads, the drawback to that tho was the amount of ' Sunday driver's ' hogging the middle lane of the motorway '. Now they never used to bother me like they do now, I would usually tailgate and intimidate them until they moved, but having changed the BMW for a Peugeot, it's not quite the same, doesn't feel quite right, and with plenty of time to make it down south, I decided to just go with the flow. As was the case on our last journey down, Helena had of course forgotten something, conveniently announcing it just as we were close to the retail park we stopped off at last time. My face lit up tho when she appeared to be heading into the Ann Summers shop, unfortunately, she opted for the Primark next door ⚫ . This did provide me with a little entertainment. Whilst we were at the checkout, the lady next to us, I'll call her Karen, was wanting to buy a multipack of knickers. She wanted to know why they were non refundable should they not fit !!! Saying that she would have tried them on in store if allowed, over the ones she was currently wearing!!! Proper arguing that it was morally wrong that she wouldn't be offered a refund should they not fit, that with the current cost of living, she could ill afford to waste money and that they should change their policy to suit her !!! Can you imagine how she'd have acted if she opened up a packet of what she assumed to be ' fresh thongs ' only to be greeted with a previously ' tried on pair ' complete with ' slug trail ' and ' eau de Harry Ramsden ' !!!! (no pinch of salt required here, this is gospel)

We were soon back on track, and I at least now had some socks for the week and Helena had 6 new pair's of pajamas, 2 pair's of slippers, a Mickley Mouse dog bowl for each dog and 6 rolls of Christmas wrapping paper.

It took us another hour to reach Southampton. Upon seeing Virtuosa I heard a very faint ' scream of joy ' from my left, fortunately for me, whilst Helena was getting a Starbucks when we stopped, I put wotsit in each ear as a sound barrier, I knew from last year she'd do it, and I didn't want perforated ear drums again. They also drowned out the ' Gangster Rap 'that Niall (son) insists we listen to on any journey!!! I'm fluent in street talk and can identify any Juice Wrld,

Lil TJ or SkiMask the SlumpGod track in an instant. Big up me ⬤

At the ship, and first little issue arises. No print out of the parking permit. I leave Helena 30 jobs to do, and she fails on one !!! I dunno !!! She wasn't the only one, there was a queue of cars, all off whom the wife hadn't printed the permit. I quickly showed them my email confirmation and we were soon parked up, car unpacked and making our way to check in some 2 hours early. This wasn't a problem, and we were onboard within 20 minutes. We quickly found our room, it's an easy ship to navigate, especially having been on her before. We dumped the bags, let Niall off to go meet up with his pals (a Snapchat group had been organised a month prior to sailing, so he had already made lot's of new friends) and headed off to get ourselves a bite to eat and a drink. As it was Sunday, we took ourselves off up to the buffet and had roast beef and yorkies ●.. yes it was busy, but it's day one, folk have travelled all day to be here, some day and night. We were seated and eating within a few minutes. Certainly not like the mass gathering of ' Druids at Stonehenge on The Summer Solstice ' that some of the recent bad reviews would like us to believe. Please don't believe those reviews, take a chance yourself. All filled up, we dragged ourselves back to the cabin. The luggage had by now arrived, so we decided to unpacked together. I took the toothbrushes into the bathroom, and whilst there, decided to evacuate my dinner, this took longer than expected, tho once I'd finished the suitcases were miraculously unpacked ● every cloud has a silver lining ●

Neither of us could really be arsed with getting dolled up for the evening, so we just went casual down to minuetto, our allocated restaurant. We had a table allocated for 7 people, and were looking forward to

mingling with the guests we expected would join us. We were halfway through dinner when it dawned on us that the empty seats would not be filled, they were obviously, one for our Niall, the others for my Mom, Stepdad and the boy's whom couldn't make the trip !!! Dohhhh....
Dinner was fine, I had a starter of tomato and basil soup. My main was ribeye steak (rare ●) with a chimmichurri sauce (sounds like a Chelsea centre forward) and a sticky toffee pudding and ice-cream for my dessert. Helena had a salad, a pasta dish and a lovely lemon sorbet to finish ●
We then had a wonder around the galleria shops, carefully browsing at all we can't afford ●, and while in one of them, I was spotted by my first fan ● Ade ● along with his family. Quite like my new found fame ●, I'll be happy to sign autographs ●.
Talking of fame, I know there's a film crew onboard and a few celebrities (allegedly), they too can have my autograph ● maybe I'll get a part in whatever they're filming, and I'll then be on my way to a 'Hollywood Walk of Fame Star ', as well as my 'Purlitzer Prize for literacy '
●.
Day done, off to bed for a well deserved sleep ●
For those onboard now, or future travellers, I've a new game to play... celebrity spotting. It can be a ' real ' celebrity or someone who ' looks like a celebrity '. Bonus points for pics of them ●
I'm certain I've seen Carl Frotch (Boxer), I'd try for a pic, but I don't want to upset him, it could end in fisticuffs, I wouldn't wanna have to spark him out ●.....

Daisy duck, sat close by to me at the bar. If it wasn't Daisy, then someone who's clearly upset the last of the summer wasps and been stung on the lips ⚫

Butter Watch..
Breakfast :- N/A
Lunch :- Judy Garland
Dinner :- Grace Jones.....

Day 2
It feels so good to be back ⚫. Have had to address an issue already tho. Had a problem hearing, and a nasty smell coming from my ears ⚫, only forgot to remove the wotsits didn't I, bright orange and very cheesy, no wonder I was getting weird looks in the lift ⚫
After a great night's sleep, beds are super comfy, we headed down to symphony restaurant for breakfast, very good it was, with, happy to report, no bent knives. Today was a sea day, so it's always a good opportunity to familiarise yourself with the ship. As it's our 2nd time on her, we're pretty up to speed, so didn't find it necessary to dig out the Karrimor boots and full North Face attire, opting for the quite British look of Shorts, T-shirt, sliders and socks combo ⚫, they're not the easiest to walk about in, but I hold all the speed and distance records on this boat, so I didn't need to worry there, plus my trainers are hanging from the ships mast,

Helena thought it was those that were giving off the cheesy odour ●

During our little meander around, we found a store that somehow had previously eluded us, not that it bothered me, but Helena was keen to check it out, so that's what we did. It was a jewellery store that sells high end, one off pieces, so I already knew that it's out of our league. The sales guy tho, he clearly thought better ● and who was I to burst his bubble. He probably knew that there's a film crew and a boxer on board, he quite obviously thought I was the boxer ●. He could see Helena had taken fancy to a silver necklace with a yellow (apparently VERY rare) diamond hanging from it. He very quickly insisted that she try it on. " oooh, this peace is made for you darling, simply stunning " he blarterd out in his pitch to sell it to me ●

He could see I was unmoved, so explained how VERY rare it was, that it had been mined in a very SPECIAL mine, that normally only sells it's diamonds to royalty, but made a special deal with MSC !!! Still I stood my ground, and I hadn't even been told the price :-).... so to humour him, and give Helena a glimmer of hope, I asked him " how much? "....... £3k !!! The diamond, was the size of a grain of rice !!

" but my friend, I can do you very good price " he kindly told me whilst punching away on his calculator. " £1700 for you today, look how radiant your stunning wife looks in it " he confidently told me. He wasn't wrong. " ill have a think about it pal, it's only day one, we tend to wait until the last day before we buy " I told him. That's when he really made us feel extra special. " OK, OK " he said

in his most confident drivell yet, " as it's you, and because I know you really want it, today only, I'll give you my own personal credit allowance as extra off, I shouldn't do this, but you're both so special to me now, it will be my honor "
I was truly moved. I asked him " would cash buy it ? "
" of course, just for you, absolutely " he replied.
Helena's eyes lit up, as did ' Ryland's ' (not his name, but reminded me of him)
" we'll be back after lunch, I'll grab my cash from the wallet " I let him know
As we left, Helena whispered into my ear that maybe we could skip lunch, and pop back to the cabin for an hour whilst Niall was out of the way ●, not gonna argue with that am I ●
No sooner are we in the cabin, she's on me like a ' Tramp on Chips ' ●●●●●
5 minutes, I mean an hour later, I get myself off the bed, have a quick ' wet wipe ' and tell her to relax, as she's clearly now exhausted. I have a fidget about in the safe, before heading out of the room, telling her I'll be back soon ●
I went straight to the shops on the Galleria, found the shop selling the Swarovski crystal and got a dead ringer of the expensive necklace that Ryland was so kind to do me a deal on. The only difference was the colour. Not a problem ♦ I went off up to the kids club, got a felt tip pen from the art activities table and coloured in the ' DIAMOND ' ●.... Genius I am ● I discarded the main wrapping, took it back to the room, and told her that I'd put it away in the safe, that because it's so expensive,

she can't wear it (felt tip needs to dry) until we back home and it's added onto the insurance as a separate item ●. As I closed the safe, Helena, now recovered, invited me back into bed, an offer I declined, told her to wait a little while, don't want an asthma attack, and we are after all on the Bay of Biscay ●

After another much needed hour of recovery, we went for a pre arranged meet up in the Sky Lounge ● What an absolutely fantastic afternoon it was, so relaxing and comfortable meeting and chatting with new people ● rather disappointed that I was the only one wearing anything pineapple tho lol ●

Before the official meet up had started, we got chatting with 2 lovely ladies from Scotland. Now Scotland is very much a love of mine, so the chat always flows when I meet a jock ●. We got onto talk of wild swimming, something I love to do when North of the border. One of the ladies, last year told me how she'd swam the English Channel!!!! Blown away !!! The Channel!!! I can just about change a Channel on the TV !!! Not only that, she did it after recovering from a swimming accident that broke her back ● Superwoman for sure x hope you read this blog, you've really inspired me ● when I get home, I'm adding extra to my Sky package, that way I can go further through the channels ●

Tonight's dinner was the Gala dinner. A chance to suit and boot ● something I don't often do, but actually like to do.

I had a starter of oxtail consommé, a main of Beef Wellington with baked alaska to follow. Helena skipped the starter. For main she had duck in an orange sauce, her first time trying duck (Good job I proof read this part, it put Dick instead of duck lol 🫠). Her pudding was an after eight inspired mouse/cake combo ... all very nice.

We then had an hour relaxing and people watching down at the infinity bar, where again, we met and chatted to some wonderful people; on the whole, cruisers are fantastic folk.

Next it was a favourite of mine, a silent disco ✨🎧♥. Not gonna lie, took a little while to get a couple set of headphones, the ship is super busy, but I'm glad we did wait it out, it was an absolutely amazing evening, the place was absolutely buzzing, young and old, all in their finest dress, singing and dancing without a care in the world 🌍. This is where I find MSC truly delivers. An exceptional night. We stuck it out til the end 🎉. After it finished, it was a quick dash up to the buffet for a few late night snacks, pizza for me, cakes and biscuits for Helena. Certainly hit the spot 😋. As we were still on the Bay of Biscay, and both very tired, we called it a night. I think Niall rolled in about 2am 😴, he loves this ship, and the freedom we allow him when onboard.

Celebrity spotting...

Carl Frotch again, and confirmed, so hopefully he doesn't read my first blog, don't really want him leaving hear bruised and battered 😅 He may well be the ' COBRA ' 🐍 but I'm the ' ANACONDA ', Helena will confirm that 😏

Claire Sweeney, looks smoking hot, I'm wondering if she's a fan of pineapple 🍍

Please PLEASE if anyone can tag either of them, I'd love them to join in the fun :-) 🔴
Frotcy can rest easy, I'm a few weight categories above him, so wouldn't rumble 🔴

Butter Watch...
Breakfast :- Her Royal Highness, The Princess of Wales, Kate ...
Lunch :- N/A
Dinner :- Mary Poppins 🔴

Day 3.....

Hi de hi cruisers 🔴 I hope I find you well on this fine day. I'd like to say I'm fine, but I'm not. I'm nursing a bit of an injury 🔴
Let's just say there will be one less squishy pineapple 🍍 for my pineapple hunt, it's now not fit for purpose having been inserted where no squishy pineapple should ever be inserted. Let's just say wifey didn't appreciate me exposing our sex life to the whole world (hoping she doesn't subscribe to our ' only fans ' page) I shall however be easier to recognise, I'm moving around on all fours, it helps ease the discomfort and is punishment from Helena 🐎
For brekky today we decided upon the buffet, which, I have to say, never let's me/us down. One of my favourites up there at breakfast time is the corned beef hash 🔴 it looks most unappealing, somewhat like the inside of my legs when I've ' chub rub ', but I can assure

those whom are put off by it's look, it's really nice, especially complimented with a nice runny egg 🥚 🥚
Today was the first port day, with La Rochelle the destination. Knowing beforehand that we have 2 French ports and 2 Spanish one's, I've been learning the lingo by watching some classic re runs of ' only fools and horse's ' and ' Fawlty Towers ". I'm now well up to speed with my finest Del Boy French and Manuel Spanish
So off the boat we go, Niall not wanting to join us, so just the 2 of us again, plus another 4k looking at the queue for the coach, you could clearly see it was a freebe, it was like an audition for Alton Tower's but no ' Wicker Man ' at the end, tho the driving made it a close match. Once we got into the town tho, we were very happy we'd made the effort. Very charming little harbour with a nice atmosphere 🍺 didn't once see any French guy's in striped shirts, necklace of onions, selling baguettes from a basket on the front of their bikes. There was tho, the usual stores selling cheap tat at stupid money, I really don't get why people buy it. Helena did get a nice bag from one of them tho, 14 fridge magnets, 22 friendship bracelets and an original, complete with certificate of authenticity, Claude Monet painting, tho I'm questioning this, I'm certain he never painted 'Pikachu'... daughter will love it tho.
After this, we had a nice, typical French afternoon tea, lovely filled, freshly baked baguettes, got to love a sub-way 🍩
Off back to the ship we went. The queue to get the transfer back was another level, very much like a primark at Christmas 🎄,

Not that it bothered me, I just pretended to be a French local, " petit poi's fromage frais " in my best hybrid Brummie/French accent I kept repeating as I pushed our way to the front ● worked a treat, tho I did get some funny looks once on the bus.

As we'd had eaten in town, we once again skipped lunch and spent a few hours soaking up the sun and sipping sprite (I'm still trying to do the challenge). The trouble with the sun and the drinking is the need for the toilet is x 10, so I took myself to the swimming pool, quicker than going the bog, no toilet roll required, and with so many kids onboard, always someone to blame the floater on, think I need a little more fibre in my diet ●obviously I was quick to depart. Tomorrow I'm trying the slides out, it may at some point resemble the log flume at Blackpool Pleasure Beach.

Evening was now upon us, so we got ourselves spruced up and made our way down to Minuetto again, just the 2 of us once more, Niall is off living his best life ● Tonight's dinner the best yet. Helena had an aubergine starter, I opted for onion soup. We both then decided upon the herb crust lamb, served with potato gratin and then finished off with a limoncello and a chocolate praline dessert respectively. Helena doesn't always finish her meals, and not one to waste, I usually finish hers off. Today was no exception, except that she literally threw the plate at me, spraying my nice new white Burberry t-shirt with mint sauce and gravy !!! Just hope the market stall back home still have some left. After dinner we decided to hunt down Niall and his homies, just to check he was still alive, and hadn't fell overboard whilst off his face on RedBull ribena. We quickly found him, with another 2 lads, and a dozen girl's, so we were quickly ushered away before we became ' those embarrassing parents ' !!! As if I would. Dunno how long it took before he found the pineapple 🍍 sticker I'd slapped on his back when saying goodbye. (Funnily enough, when he rolled in at 2am he said some woman had invited him back to the yacht club!)

Knowing he was safe, we went and spent the evening up in the adult only sky lounge. It's an absolutely fantastic venue, looking out over the ship, which looks even more amazing in it's night time glow. We were soon joined by some more fantastic people, 2 of whom were teacher's (I'd like this blog teacher graded please, I was crap at school, so getting some good grades will make my parents very proud, they both get to see these ⚫). We genuinely loved your company, I'd imagine you are both the ' cool teacher's ' in school. As I've mentioned a few times already, the majority of folk on these cruises 🍸 are awesome ⚫ those in the minority, who like to pick and moan, maybe try and make a little more effort, interact, I promise you, you'll be a better person for it, and u don't even need pineapples ⚫ both Helena and myself look forward to meeting and mingling again this cruise with you, and any others who care to join us ⚫

Upon departure from there, we grabbed ourselves a couple drinks and the now obligatory slice of 🍕 pizza, a great going to bed snack. Scoffed that down and hit the

sac, and was out like Carl Frotch will be if we ' get it on '
●

No celebrity's of note yesterday, real or lookalikes.
Tho Shayne Ward is onboard, I wouldn't have a scooby
what he looks like.

Butter watch
Breakfast :- Gal ' wonder woman ' Gadot
Lunch :- N/A
Dinner :- Emma ' baby spice ' Bunton

Day 4
 already!! How did that happen??? !!
Another day, another port, today's calling, Bilbao.
Breakfast this morning was a trip to the buffet, and was
on my one's, both Niall, the only time I see him, and
Helena were still in a deep slumber, so I decided to
leave them be. There's been, and there still popping up
on the page, lot's of negativity regarding the buffet and
the food, that it's like a cattle market, never anywhere to
sit.... Well that's ABSOLUTELY not the case. There is
plenty of choice, I'd go as far as saying an abundance of
choice, that caters for all. Jesus (father, son & holy
spirit, not the Arsenal one) managed to feed the
masses on a bit of fish, a few cobs (barms, baps,
stotties, rolls) and a couple bottles of lambrini, so be
thankful, be grateful and keep it real. I say keep it real,
as most of those who pipe up with their complaints are

those who are happy to grab a tesco £3 meal deal, or a scollop and chips to eat at their desk or on the back of the no.23 bus !!! You could always pop your towel on a table the night before to reserve it ●....
There may well not be any Arbroath Smokies, or Manx Kippers, and sometimes the banana's are a tad green, so be it......
Anyway, I had a full English, bostin it was.
As I'm a good Husband and Dad, I decided I'd take the sleeping beauties back some breakfast in bed. Carrying 2 plates and 2 drinks from deck 15 to deck 5 is by no means an easy feat, it's a good job I'm ' all man ' , it made pressing the button for the lift a breeze ●. Not so easy gaining access to the room tho, but a couple of boot's to the door and I was soon in, tho to a rather unfriendly reception. They then had the cheek to moan at what I'd got them. A breadstick for Niall, a pancake for Helena and probably half a cuppa tea each, spilt most of it when booting the door. Told them there was nothing up in the buffet, little choice and massive queues, and to count themselves lucky as I got nothing ●
While they fannied around getting themselves ready I felt the need to ' drop the kids at the pool '. As I was already in the cabin, and the slides not yet open, I took the traditional option and delivered them safely down the poodrobe. There's something I don't like when sat in here tho. The mirror placement. There's me sat there, minding my own business, but when I glance up, there's x 3 of me staring back, proper freaks me out. Even worse when getting out the shower, I thought for a minute that the pineapples had worked and there was

me plus 3 in all our glory, don't think Helena would have been happy or able lol...

No coach was necessary for today, just behind the ships docking is a nice little beach and a few shops. Niall even decided to join us as I think most of his friends were going on shore, and he wanted to seek out a new vape. So we headed out and went to the shops first, tho most were still closed, not like back home, they pick and choose their hours here, no continuity. Anyway, we did manage to find him a vape, so happy him. Now mission completed, we took a nice stroll on the beach, but didn't stay to long, as there appeared to be a mist/fog rolling in. Clearly that wasn't the case, it was just Niall doing his best Thomas The Tank Engine impression, creating his very own ozone layer hole.

Weather was roasting, so getting back on, we decided it was to be a pool lounge day. While looking for a bed that hadn't had a towel on it since the Roman Times, we bumped into our new found friends, Marilyn and Keith, who happened to have a couple loungers free, so we joined them. I was also the hero of the day for Keith. He hadn't planned for such nice weather, so was sat sweating his tits off in a pair of jeans, so I saved the day and offered him a pair of spare shorts I'd got, I did think to offer my budgie smuggler's, but I'm saving them for white night 🌑 they were just the ticket for him, and were a perfect match for the lovely pineapple 🍍 shirt he combo'd them with 🌑 We spent the afternoon chatting amongst ourselves, and had an excellent time, picking out those deserving of the pineapple stickers that are soon to make there appearance lol.

Spotted Carl Frotch again while sunbathing, wouldn't even glance my way, bricking it I'm guessing 🔴
Didn't really bother with lunch again today, we more grazed and picked, and all had a free ice cream curtesy of Niall, apparently the minors drink package includes it
Before we left we arranged to meet up after dinner up in the Sky Lounge.
Dinner once again was taken by just the 2 of us in Minuetto, Niall doesn't like the fancy stuff. Both had soup starters and steak for main, tho mine wasn't the best I've had, it was still perfectly palatable, and the Diane sauce it was served with was really nice. My pudding was a white chocolate cake, really good, Helena had a cinnamon rice pudding that unfortunately was served stone cold, maybe that's how the Italian's roll !!
As we were leaving the dining room, we spotted the 2 lovely Scottish ladies we met the other day, so we joined them for half hour, having an absolute ball, especially when the clicked I was ' pineapple man '
We are meeting and making so many friends on this cruise 🔴
We then took ourselves up into the Sky Lounge for an absolutely brilliant night, once again meeting with new people, and joined by our new found friends. What an absolutely fantastic venue with awesome company, sharing our life stories and adventures with each other. Look forward to this daily now 🔴. With this, I reiterate to those who are questioning MSC, please don't, this is an

absolutely amazing ship, with amazing guests and staff. Remember, YOLO, make it count........

Celebrity watch today....
Jennifer Aniston's body, didn't see the boat race for confirmation 🔴

Butter Watch :-
Breakfast :- Elsa (the ice Queen)
Lunch :- N/A
Dinner :- Lana Rhodes (if u know, u know)

Watch for details on pineapple 🍍 hunt 🔴

There once was a couple at sea
Sailing on board MSC
They hid pineapples around
In the hope they'd be found
To take home as a cruise memory.....

We shall hide them tonight
Whilst all are asleep
Go seek out tomorrow
Your pineapple treat 🔴

Karen's are sour
Pineapples sweet
Find one of me
And you're in for a treat

Place me outside your room
Upside down if you dare
There's fun to be had
If you're willing to share 🍍......

Day 5
🍍 🍍 the penultimate port day. La Coruna.
A different kind of start to the day today. No breakfast for a change, nothing out the normal when at home, think holiday makes me greedy, I'm certain I've eaten the daily intake of a hippopotamus, my belly tells me that I have, so it certainly caused no harm to skip a meal. Helena and Niall followed suit, tho not through choice, they were both still sleeping 🍍 if I don't wake them, then they ain't getting up, and the pounds they've added so far this trip, they won't exactly be wasting away.
Weather had taken a turn, raining and blowing a gale, so that confined us to the ship. This wasn't a major issue, it's a port we have frequented before, and I didn't want to have to pull Helena off the statue that welcomes you outside the port, she can never resist giving it a rub for luck, I wouldn't mind but i was the original model for said statue, she's the real deal at home and never wants to give it a rub for luck 🍍
So, as we were ship bound for the day, Helena suggested we try some new things 🍍, I got more than

excited at this suggestion, but was quickly brought back to earth ● when she told me she'd signed us up for some line dancing. Now I love the ' Gavin & Stacey ' episode with the line dancing, but no, not for me sorry. Now if she wanted to do ' Dirty Dancing ' then absolutely no problem, I got them moves, I taught Patrick ● tho I'd have worried about the lift at the end with the timber she's added this trip ● would have made a great ' You've Been Framed ' clip, sure to have bagged me the £250 prize ●

What we did instead was plan, with military precision the very important and much anticipated ' operation pineapple hunt ' We prepared the goodies and strategically planned exactly where we were planting the main prizes and we jotted down a little message on the back of some of the stickers we were to hide. This we combined with lunch at the buffet, safety tucked away in a corner seat, so as not to give the game away, I even had to don a disguise as I'm getting recognised more and more ● tho wearing one of Helena's dresses whilst sporting a fairly thick beard got me a few odd lucks and rather bizarrely a pinch on the bum ●

With the planning finished, it was time to get ready for white night ☽ ●. Now we've all 3 been looking forward to this for a long time, and have had our outfits ready for week's, tho I ' wasn't allowed ' my outfit of choice, apparently dressing as an ' IMPERIAL STORMTROOPER ' would make me look a prat !!! I think it's more because I wouldn't let her dress as ' OLAF ', I was worried the carrot would go mouldy.

So we donned the outfits we had and went down for dinner. Again, we chose Minuetto. We both had soup starters and a roast beef dinner for main, I had ice-cream for dessert, Helena an apple strudel. Quite possibly the hardest dinner I've ever eaten. This was because we were on the Bay of Biscay, which on previous cruises (minus the little bedroom accident on recent trip down to a rogue wave) has been kind to us. Not tonight!!! No, it decided to throw up gale force winds and an 8 meter swell. Eating a roast, that's drowning in gravy whilst wearing nothing but white is no mean feat, but somehow, we survived unscathed, no nasty brown stains thank God ●...... After we finished eating, it's now become customary to pop over and have a catch up with our new found Scottish friends, the lovely Shona & Dawn ● we love our little meet ups, and very much look forward to keeping in touch, I'm a frequent visitor to Jockland, so I'll message u to get the kettle on someday when passing through.

Oh, did I say we come through unscathed??? Well, up to the point we left the dinner room we had. But then, out of nowhere.... blurrrhhh.... I was hit, like a tramp hits the bottle, out of nowhere with sea sickness ●, something I've never had on my previous cruises, and something I hope doesn't become recurrent ● Helena, no problem, Niall no problem, this I'm grateful for. Unfortunately for me, it put the brakes on white night for me ● I had no choice but to take my sorry arse to bed ●

Thankfully, Helena and Niall did get to join in, and both had an absolutely epic time, I spent the night in a semi comatose state, luckily in bed and not hugging the bog.

Celebrity of the day, a kind of hybrid mix of Mick Hucknall crossed with Robert Plant.
Butter Watch :-
Breakfast :- N/A
Lunch :- Mary Berry
Dinner :- Ru Paul

Day 6
Definitely the day after the night before ●
Somehow I survived the night without recreating ' that ' scene from The Exorcist, and, thanks to Helena's ingenuity, I was cleverly kept in the bed with her placing a filled suitcase either side of me, securing me to them with some pink fluffy hand cuffs and leg restraints, and kept quiet with a ball gag gimp mask. I knew they'd come in handy ● the butt plug saved rear end embarrassment too ● you can never be over packed for a cruise. For me, breakfast was off the menu, just a few gallons of water to take away the taste from the pvc the mask was made of, clearly not the advertised leather wish said it was !!! Thankfully, the sea had somewhat calmed down, still on the choppy side, but much more manageable today, praise the Lord. A few paracetamol and 6 packets of Rennies and I was almost back firing on all cylinders. My downfall last night resulted in the placement of the pineapple 🍍 paraphernalia being delayed a little, so we put them out before lunch. I think

quite a lot of folk may have had a rough night and treated themselves to a lie in, as it was fairly quiet all around the ship, so the stealth placement went as planned and un noticed, tho Helena attracted a few choice looks whilst she placed one underneath the Buddha/Sumo wrestler up in the Sky Lounge, looking like she was giving it an enema ● I even think it winked ● at her lol ●

Lunch was taken up at the buffet, where I today set up my camera, taking a time-lapse video of ' The Cattle Market ' that ' Never ' has any seating/plates/bowls/cutlery/food etc.... think my video will end that myth for good I hope. Didn't have much to eat, I didn't want to chance it, we still had a fair few hours of The Bay Of Biscay to negotiate, and mother nature can change things in an instant. After lunch, we met up with our friends and partook in a quiz in the Carousel Theatre at the back of the ship. I've done a lot of quizzes in my time, I'm quite the vat of useless information, but this was another level of hard, I think ' The Eggheads ' would have struggled. It was guess the movie production company from their opening musical intros, really difficult ●, managed 4 out of 15, Helena, somehow managed 6 !!! Met another fan here, even wanted a selfie with me ● I will keep a lookout on the page for it.

Quiz done, we spent the remainder of the afternoon in the cabin, sorting out the clothes and shoes we'd need for the remainder of the cruise, packing away the washing and the ones we wouldn't require. Makes for an easier tomorrow night 🌙

Excellent evening dinner once again at Minuetto, I again set up my camera to capture a Time-lapse, you'll see just how attentive and hard working the staff are, and how quickly the food is served, I've heard wait times of over 30 minutes, which (not calling any Karen's a liar) seem not accurate to me, especially as this is, I believe, the busiest cruise on this ship since pre ' just a cold '..... I had soup, lasagne and tiramasu, Helena lamb chops and tiramasu, be careful of this, I inhaled the cocoa from the top, almost coughing my spleen out !! We once again had a catch up with our favourite Scots, before taking ourselves for an evening in the champagne 🎙 bar . Another great evening with our new friends, and recognised again by a few approving fans 🔴 am I allowed to call them fans lol 🔴
Late into the evening, I popped off to check in on Niall, absolutely fine, loving life. On the way back through the Atrium, I copped ' Elvis ' , never been a fan, but the guy was fantastic, had the crowd in his hands 🔴 kudos to him. Managed to then fight my way back through the crowd to the champagne bar, and told our crew that we needed to join the ' Hollywood Hits Party ' , and so glad we did, an absolutely brilliant end to the day, singing and dancing in an immense atmosphere 🔴
What a simply magnificent cruise. The obvious only gutting part is that my Mom, Stepdad and the Foster boy's aren't here with us, all the more reason for another 🔴

Celebrity Watch :- Heston Blumenthal

Butter Watch :-
Breakfast :- N/A
Lunch :- Any of Charlie's Angels
Dinner :- Sandra Bullock

Day 7 (finally)
Final full day 🌑, can't believe it. But all good things
must come to an end, so they say, and this trip has
certainly lived up too, and beyond my expectation.
Started the day with breakfast in the Symphony
restaurant 🌑, very attentive service, and a nice way to
start the day, tho I was all on my own again, left the
sleeping beauties to it, and to be fair to then, it was
pretty early that I rose. Not to early for a ' Karen ' tho !!!
Wanting her eggs benedict with the sauce on the side,
which is fair enough. Obviously it arrives as a normal
one, so sends it back. New one arrives, no sauce,
again, she moans, and has a valid point. They quickly
go get the hollandaise to rectify, so alls well that ends
well..... strange thing was, she didn't touch the sauce at
all, not even a cheeky dip !! 🌑
My full English was spot on 🌑 I then ordered eggs
benedict to take back to the room for sleepy head. 🌑
Le Havre today, very strange they would name a place
after the guy who shot JFK !! Not exactly politically
correct is it !!! Weather upon arrival was damp and moist
(trigger words intentionally lol) so we didn't bother

leaving the ship, we made the most of our last day onboard. Most of this morning was spent having a wonder around the ship with my camera in hand, filming as many of the various places on offer, I shall edit and upload as soon as I can 🔘
We had a final lunch up in the buffet, which was, as always busy, but as always manageable and excellent food 🔘 I'm gonna miss margarita pizza with veal stew and a side of spinach pasty 🔘

Greetings all, thought it about time I did a review of my simply magnificent Virtuosa cruise, 16/23 October (La Rochelle, Bilbao, La Coruna and Le Havre). I like to refer to this as ' The Pineapple 🍍 Cruise '
My hope is that this review, will once and for all, allay any fears you may have, most likely, embedded into you by the ' Karen's/Kevin's/Snowflakes ' out there. If it's your first time cruising on Virtuosa, then leave that fear back home. If you've been on her before, then you, like myself, know you're in for a treat.
The boarding process, often a sore subject, and a favourite of the snowflakes, they obviously like to ' start as they mean to go on ' ; Asked a guy (we'll call him Mr Burton 🔘 to protect him) what he thought:-
" Never before in the history of the world,
Had such a mass of human beings moved and suffered together.
This was no disciplined march, it was a stampede,
Without order and without a goal, six million people unarmed and unprovisioned driving headlong.

It was the beginning of the rout of civilization, of the massacre of mankind.

A vast crowd buffeted me towards the already packed ship.

I looked up enviously at those safely on board... straight into the eyes of my beloved wife.

At sight of me she began to fight her way along the packed deck to the gangplank.

At that very moment, it was raised,

And I caught a last glimpse of her despairing face as the crowd swept me away from her.

To be honest, think he was quite grateful to have broken away from her and their 11 children, both set's of Grandparents, Aunts, Uncles and countless cousins....

He was obviously one of those who had a boarding time of 4pm that arrived at 9.30am !!! Now, I've no issue with early arrival, when it's maybe an hour or so early, we were an hour ahead of schedule, but don't take the p*#s and then have the audacity to moan.

From parking, to pizza in hand, we were on in 25 minutes, kudos to MSC, very pain free and efficient. Just remember to print off your documents and have your passport to hand.

Our room of choice this time around was an outside cabin on deck 5. Great choice for 3 of us. Plenty enough room, for what is essentially a place to sleep 😴 and a place to get dressed. Ample storage, a hairdryer for the ladies or posers, and a decent shower with provided shower gel and shampoo, conditioner can be requested if needed. For anything else you may require a bedroom for, I suggest looking for rooms that have a pineapple 🍍

displayed on the door ● (these are not available to pre book beforehand, you seek out once onboard) you'll find them most accommodating, most refreshing not to not be greeted with the old ' not tonight, I've got a headache ' reply. Sadly, I never did find one of them room's, guessing they all in the yacht club ●.

Now onto the eating ● and drinking :-
You'll want for nothing.
We'll talk buffet first. At times, yes it's busy, think Primark on giro day. But time it right (it's pretty much open 18 hours) and you'll be fine. They always have a roast dinner, there's always your ' kids staples ' of chips, nuggets, burgers, hotdogs etc.... The star of the show tho, has to be the pizza ◀ cooked fresh, morning, noon and night, and it's absolutely gorgeous. Onboard they make their own mozzarella, and it pays dividends, they never scrimp on the topping, it's genuinely the best pizza ever, they even do a charcoal crust for the artisan of you, and a cheese less one for the vegans to enjoy. Now talking vegan, the on display choices are not massive, but speak to the chefs, and they will accommodate you, vegetarian choices aplenty, so, as said, nobody will go hungry.
Those on a drink package, waiting staff are plentiful and will take your orders and bring to your table, occasionally you may wait 5 minutes for it to arrive, but I never experienced longer. Those not on any drink package, I expect few and far, you can always get tea, coffee, hot chocolate, various juices and water from the numerous dispensers dotted around up here, tho you

will have to self serve them. I could happily manage without a drink package, I don't drink alcohol, neither does the bread knife, it's definitely doable, and can save you a few bob ⚫

Your included restaurant :-

We were placed in Minuetto for our ' posh dining ' and ate there every evening. Obviously more formal than the buffet. Apart from the official ' elegant night ' there's no real dress code, tho we find it nice to spruce ourselves up (could be pineapple fans checking us/u out). It makes a nice change from the normal, where i ' might wear classic Reeboks, knackered Converse or tracky bottoms tucked in socks ' ..... The food in here is also up a few levels, tho they do occasionally have odd things married together. And remember, if you don't like something, your waiter will happily get you something else from the menu, and there's always the buffet after should you feel the need. There's always a vegetarian option, and they always have, you may need to request (we asked to see it as travelling with 2 next year) a vegan menu. Once again, don't listen to those moaning about quality and wait times, these are the people that are happy to wait an hour for a kebab at Binley Mega Chippy at midnight after a few to many lambrini's and a toke on ' Delroys ' finest herb 🌿. You'll love it, and feel a great sense of well-being, especially if you interact with your waiting staff, and fellow guests.

Let's talk bars now. There's lots of them, all popular. What I find mental is those ordering a ' bloody mary ' or an ' orgasm ' at 9 am. Now the latter would have been delivered the previous night x 3 in my room ⚫, and maybe a redbull would be required for recovery purposes, but the need to turn into the ' winos outside tesco express ' when on holiday baffles me. Pace yourselves a little, there's some fantastic coffees and hot chocolate to die for at the bars, all included in your drink package. On colder / wet days and evening's, seats are at a premium, but be patient and you'll get your reward, and they no different to bars and clubs on dry land, far to many people become ' entitled/ privileged on holiday. Service is always first class, the bartenders work very VERY hard, as do the waiters. A useful tip would be not to let your glass run empty, it's not rocket science ● Entertainment. Well this is a party ship for sure. It comes alive around 10.30pm, and it's absolutely amazing. The themed nights especially brilliant. The buzz and atmosphere in the Galleria, the heart of Virtuosa at night is electric, and if you let down your hair, leave your troubles behind, you'll have the time of your life. It's amazing to see the young and the old dancing and singing their hearts out, living their best lives ♥ A must is the silent disco !!! What an experience, well worth the inevitable wait to get the headphones ● And do not miss white night, it's amazing the effort the guests and staff put in, just be careful with your gravy at dinner, MSC cannot be held responsible for any spoon spills ● Daily entertainment is plentiful too. Be it having fun in the pools (salt water, makes perfect eco sense, slightly heated) or chilling in the hot tubs (normal chlorine and lovely and warm) enjoying epic panoramic views when docked or at sea. There's a brilliantly equipped Gym for the Instagramers to help keep in ' ship shape '.

Loads for teenagers, including a 5 a side/ basketball hall, apparently it's been graced by KSI and the sidemen!!! A bowling alley, and an arcade with 2 formula 1 simulators, a tip for this would be to purchase, before you travel, a fun pass. At the time I got mine, it was £80 for £140 value. Also, add a cap to any under 18's cruise card, as left uncapped they can and do (£420 in one evening at the arcade) go over the limit if not capped) For the younger kids, there's a lego station onboard and an array of clubs that parents can dump the kids off at for a few hours.

The best part, especially in the summer months, for all kid's and adults, is the aquapark and high ropes up on the top desk 🌑 ,it's sometimes easy to forget your in the middle of the ocean on a ship 🌑 simply magnificent. Adults can also enjoy an ' Adults only ' bar , the sky lounge, it's a great atmosphere and brilliant for making new friends 🌑. There's also a casino, tho I'm not a gambling man myself, it was fun on the last evening to use the money we had left over for a bit of fun, wife ended up winning £100 🌑 The only drawback here for me, it's a smoking area too 🌑, as a non smoker, I didn't like it, but it's not a complaint, I've obviously got the choice.

Showtime... can't actually comment on this, we've yet to watch one, we to busy with everything else lol, tho I've only ever heard good things, so I'd guess, if you've the time, give them a go.

I'll wrap it up now, I tend to drivel on 🌑

I'm more than happy to answer questions, I can do serious when required, but I love to add a little humour, remember life's to short, live it and love it, laugh along the way.

My biggest tip would be to interact. Myself, my beloved wife Helena and son Niall have met some amazing people who helped make this our best cruise to date (4th)

Do share tables, do sit next to others in the bars and the lounges. Dance the night away. Leave your worries on dry land. YoLo

And be careful with them pineapples 🍍 , they do actually work...... ⚫

(I respectfully declined, nice for the ego tho)

Butter watch....
Back home now, and with it coming up to winter, we're on the Flora ⚫

Love to you all, ⚫ until the next time (Norwegian Fjords 26/08/23: should you care to join me/us onboard, or avoid lol)

⚫ peace out :-)

Everybody....yeah.......Rock your body....yeah.......Everybody.....yeah......... Rock your body right, Brady's back, alright 👍 O my god I'm back again...... OK, OK, I'll quit with the 'Backstreet Boy's' , don't wanna upset our Gaz Barlow who may or may not be onboard on our upcoming Iona cruise.

So yes, I'm back onboard, and myself along, with my beloved wifey Helena are very much looking forward to being guests once again to Pam and Ozzy on Iona, one of their 2 new ship's, we've Arvia booked for October, and are really looking forward to gaining our sea legs again 🌑.

Once again, I'll be offering my very detailed blogging for your pleasure (or displeasure if you're a snowflake ❄). Butter watch will be making a very welcome return I'm pleased to announce 🌑 as will a couple of new features 🌑.

We set sail on the 29th of this month, the day we celebrate our 28th wedding anniversary, the cruise is my gift to my beloved for putting up with me all these year's. I'm very much looking forward to seeing the gift she has for me, clocked her coming out of Ann Summers with a somewhat bulging bag last weekend, and buying cable ties, wd40 and duct tape from home bargains 🌑 just hoping that as there's no ' Bay of Biscay ' crossing on this cruise, I'll not be requiring the ' special cream ' again !!!

This will be the first of 3 cruises we've got booked this year, having very much caught the bug. That said, I've

had to settle for the lowest grade, inside cabin and no drinks package on this sailing as our 'Only Fans' page has yet to gain any subscriptions. I've not even sorted parking yet, so if any of u 'Southamptonintes' wanna let me park on your drive, I'll bring u back a keyring and a lock of Gary Barlows hair (if he's on) as a thank you ●
For those of you who will be on the aforementioned cruise, feel free to say hello, or avoid ● if u see me/us ● I'm absolutely buzzing for it, as is the bread knife, and it's ABSOLUTELY something we are both very much in need of ●. One last note, Wifey is of to church tomorrow, I've asked her to have a word with God and Jesus, in the hope he'll bless us with good weather, orcas and a late night Aurora. I'm bringing a pineapple 🍍 for any other bonuses ●●

See u all very soon xxx

It's the final countdown...de de derrrrrr derrr, de de det det derrrrrrr ,de de derrrr derr, de de det det det det derrrrrrrrrrrr.... u know how it goes :-) love me a bit of 80's rock ● .... 11 day's to go, or 10, or 9, or 8..... all depends on when u reading my drivell ●. Thought I'd try and get the juices flowing with a little pre blog, a little ' foreplay ' if u will ●
It's been a while since I sailed, October to be precise, and I'm more than ready and needing my fix, as is tge bread knife ● . Nowt was planned for this early in the year, but I kept seeing posts, and ad's, finally, at the end

of February, like a fly to sh#%, I stopped hovering over ' book now ' and actually did it. It was kind of a panic buy, as a week before booking, it was the wife's birthday, and (ungrateful 🌑 cow 🐏) she didn't like the pressie I got her, apparently a new ' 85 inch flat screen TV, complete with surround sound and an xbox series x ' wasn't top of her list, and apparently, the valentines present the previous week, wasn't suitable!!! I thought crotchless would help save a little time when peeing 🌑.... so, the cruise was a bit of a peace offering, and was very well received, the valentines present came in useful after all 🌑

It's always great motivation to have something to look forward too, and the Fjords, the destination of choice, have been on our to do list for a while now, so much so, this will be one of 2 trips there in 2023, we go on MSC virtuosa end of summer with family and friends 🌑.
This one, is also timed for our 28th wedding anniversary, so again, that valentines gift may well prove a good buy, if not, I've got my pineapple stuff already packed in my JD carrier bag...

The drawback to going in April to the Fjords, is weather... it ain't exactly bikini and short dresses weather, so obviously wife needed a complete new wardrobe. But now she's ' over the hill ' having turned the big Five'O , we can no longer shop Primark, o no!!! , Marks and Spencer, Joules and Radley are the go too's now, not so easy on the pocket I'll tell u !!! I now have to suffer the ' Lonsdale and Slazenger look from SportsDirect (will a tracksuit work for formal night?) 🌑

Still, beggars can't be choosers ● at least we're back on the water ● suppose it's a small price to pay ● This will be our 5th cruise since our very first in October 21, we've well and truly caught the bug, as mentioned, there's another Fjords trip booked end of summer, and got Arvia booked for October, so u can expect lot's more blogging from me, should the wife not throttle me ●. We're travelling down to Southampton the night before this time, booked us into a a Travelodge, give myself an extra day off work, and it's a safety net, wouldn't want the old Austin conking out on us when we've a boat to catch the same day, if it does, then please pick us up, we'll be the hitchhikers on the A34, We'll be easily recognisable, I'll be on the floor getting kicked by the wife, she wanted a Tesla and not an Allegro !!!! You can drop us at the hotel and pick us back up in the morning, just make sure you've space for all our luggage ● I'll buy you a drink onboard with the money I'll save on parking ● I've not pre booked that, there's always someone's drive I can block ●

That's enough for now, I, along with my lovely wife Helena look forward to seeing you all on board ● safe trip down xx

TFI Friday, think that's the saying ● and what a Friday it is ●, it's only holiday time, T minus 24 hours until I'm once again in the company of Pam and Ozzy, setting sail for the first time on Iona, with the bread knife Helena by my side, and joined by my Mother and Stepdad. Work completed yesterday, so I'm now ' out of office ' until ol Big Ears officially receives his crown 👑 so a nice 11 day R & R .

After the last job, I dropped my son (he sort of works with me, he keeps the passenger seat warm, and the cafe busy) to the pub, and I went and treated myself to a short back n side's, followed by a back sac and crack wax, not something I'd wish on my worst enemy, it's left me walking like Elton John on his wedding night ⚫

I then stopped off at the local car wash, to give the old Allegro the £3 wash, didn't bother with a wax, or the inside cleaning, does nothing to brown, and I'm sure it causes the rust to disintegrate. Final job of the evening was shopping for the kid's, stocking up the cupboards, the fridge and the freezer with evening they need whilst we're away. The mistake I made in doing this, was taking them along with me !!! 2 baskets full in Heron Foods, and 2 trollies full at Aldi !!! Nearly £300 lighter, a little bonus tho, I was given a quid by an old lady for one of the trollies, I'd managed to unlock it with a couple of pennies wrapped in foil ⚫ winner winner, chicken dinner ⚫

As if all that shopping wasn't enough, they demanded take out, sort of compensation for not coming on the trip, and having to dog sit !! Another £50 gone, theregoes the cable car lift trip !!! Food done, shopping

away, I had an ice bath to soothe my gooch, and wash away the debris the waxing and hair cut left, after pulling the plug, it looked like chewbacka had joined me in it. I then, finally hit the sack, and had a pretty decent night's sleep 🌑 z^{Zz}. Morning.....cuppa tea made for the beloved, it was out into the garden for me, to clear the 2 day's worth of, 3 x dog's bovril bullets that left the decking like a marmite minefield, 5 minutes later, 2 carrier bag's filled, and lot's of heaving, I was done. I lobbed it over the back gate, washed my hands in the pond, and took myself off to get dressed and load the motor up.

Motor loaded, kid's warned ▲ not to kill each other, the dog's, the cat, the fish and to remember bin day and dog shite duties, and we were off. We live in Brum, so about 140 miles from the port, so travelling the day before when we can is always a bonus, stopping off at a travelodge for the night, and treating ourselves to a meal. As Fridays go, the route down was pretty incident free, we took the M5, M42, M40, A34, M3 drive down, and are currently chilling out in Eastleigh. Had an absolutely cracking 3 course dinner, myself having BigMac, medium fries and a chocolate shake, wifey a happy meal (she got Queen Bee) followed by a McFlurry..... I'm now typing up this masterpiece, whilst wife showers and shaves, it's then an early night 🌙........ so excited for tomorrow ⚫

Sleep well folks, and look forward to the next instalment and the eagerly awaited return of BUTTER WATCH ....All being well we'll meet some of you onboard, feel free to avoid too ⚫

Yay ⚫ it's embarkation day ⚫ but I start the daily blog with a few niggles. First off the bat, I'm in the dog house. My choice of the Travelodge @ Eastleigh Central just didn't cut the mustard with the wife. It's pretty much a converted office block, with no parking and no sense of welcome. It's dark, and lacks any atmosphere. I wasn't expecting the Ritz, but for once, I can't really argue with the woman who's ' always right ' as on this occasion, she was bang on. Fingers crossed 🤞 I don't get a parking ticket, as I parked in the private car park behind in a reserved for management spot, I thought that as it's Friday, and a bank holiday weekend, that I'd be safe, and there was no sign of a ticket on the car, and no visible ANPR on entering the carpark. I've duct taped the barrier back on, and the damage to the Allegro just blends in with it's other scuffs and scrapes. As for quality of sleep, I can't answer that with any sort of real clarity, as I actually thought I was already onboard of Iona as wife had restless leg's, kicking the shite out of me !!!! Probably on purpose for picking a crap hotel.

Banging shower tho ⚫ certainly set me up for the day, nice and refreshing. Breakfast consisted of 2 jam donuts, half a packet of snack eggs and a cuppa soup I found in the bottom of my bag, must have been there since I last used it, which was a scout camp in the early 90's ⚫ I'm sure it'll be fine.....

Our kick out time was 11 am, and we duly departed on time. Our embarkation time was 2.15, so as we were ony 15 minutes away, we knew we'd have a few hours to kill. I did drive to Ocean Terminal straight away tho, to offload the luggage, which was absolutely seemless, made even easier by my ' back, sac and crack ' limp, the stewards thought I was a raspberry ripple, so helped me offload ⚫ and were most thankful of the tip of a toffee

crisp and a 50p (the new one with Charlie's mug on it)
.....
We then spun back around and dumped the car on a
quiet side street, where I stuck my mates disability pass
(hopefully he don't need it this week, i forgot to tell him
i'd took loan of it) in the front window.
As today's our 28th wedding anniversary 🖤 I treated
Helena (I'll be more formal now, she hates me referring
to her as ' The wife/ Mrs etc) to a Starbucks. Whilst we
were there, I made my excuses to ' go for a Jimmy
Riddle ' when in fact, I took myself of in search of Ann
Summers to buy a ' little something ' and a nice black
lacey number, I just hope it doesn't rub my shaving rash.
Unfortunately the ' little something ' was out of stock, so
I settled for something (not quite so little) from the
greengrocers .....
That ate up a few hours, so we headed off back to the
terminal to meet up with my Mother and Ol Man. I
helped them out with their luggage and we went off to
board. The Ol Fella is currently in a wheelchair, so I
didn't have to ' over exaggerate ' my new found
disability, as they had assisted boarding, which linked us
with them, and from joining the queue at 2pm, we were
onboard at 2.30, absolutely seamless.... but... there was
a little hitch. At the boarding process, my phone rang, it
was ships security, apparently I'd a prohibited item in my
checked luggage !!! So once onboard we had to go sort
that out !!! How was I to know blow torches were not
allowed!! I'll have to figure a different way to soften the
butter.......

First impressions of the ship were 'WOW'... she's a little bit special 💜 we're gonna have a cracking week. We quickly did muster and found our cabin, inside on this sailing, but perfectly adequate. If at some point we fancy an upgrade, I'll pack the bog with a couple of crisp bags, so it becomes unusable ⚫ works a treat apparently ⚫ We then went off to find some grub ⚫ I had fish and chips, Helena a burger and chips, very nice ⚫... knackered, we then took ourselves to the cabin for 40 winks.

This is where I'll sign off this blog, my next will be when we reach our first port, Stavanger, I forgot to set up a GoFund me to help pay for the Internet onboard, so I will only get online in ports.....

Weather has been and still is fantastic, so looks like we're in for a nice passage though the Solent, the Channel and North Sea....

Butter Watch will make it's triumphant return in my next installment ⚫

Peace and love to you all, happy anniversary to my beloved and happy sailings to us and all onboard....next stop Norway 🏴 💜

Day one proper, sea day, and a very pleasant day. Woke about 8am, which is a lie in for me, after a good night's sleep. We're in an inside cabin on this adventure, a first for us, and I've zero complaints, it's more than adequate and I like the dark at night ⚫. As it was our first brekky, we opted for one of the MDR's, as I wanted to properly test the butter for the triumphant return of butter watch, which today I've included an explanation as to what it exactly is for those not in the know. I opted for the P&O breakfast, and cocked up a bit, forgot to add beans and there was no liver on it like there was/is on Ventura, maybe it's something I can ask for, I love it, especially accompanied with a nice runny egg, a much better marriage than with faver beans and a nice chianti...... Helena had her favourite eggs benedict, looked lovely, but a double portion was to much for her. We shared a table with 2 other couples, which is something I like doing, I love interaction and chatting with others, and it made for a very nice morning.

After breakfast, we went upon the top deck at the back of the ship, Helena doing some crosswords and me scanning the water with my binoculars. I did think I saw whales, but soon remembered we are on the opposite coast, it was probably Norwich or Great Yarmouth 👍

For lunch, we met up with my Mother, my step dad didn't fancy coming out, so we ate at the buffet. I had what was described as a chicken korma, but was in no way such, for one, not a hint of coconut, and two, it was a bit spicy, something I can't manage, a polo mint is too spicy for me, tho I'd be happy with the spice girls, except posh.....

After lunch we spent a few hours up in the crow's nest, there were no crow's. I tried myself to do a crossword that I picked up from one of the bar's, way above my level, so I just filled it with swear words and profanity ●

The evening was celebration night, so knowing it would take Helena 4 hours to get ready we spent the afternoon in the cabin, her sorting herself out, I watched the football, and got my first Norway fix, Haaland bagging a penalty, taking Man City back top of the league ⚫ For celebration night, we dined in opal with the folks, and had a lovely evening, I had the amusing bush, a duck starter, chicken chowder for the soup course and a main of fillet steak with asparagus and a red wine jus, tho I left the asparagus, apparently it leaves a bitter taste later on ⚫.....pudding, I ate both mine and Helena's, I was fit to burst, as were my trousers and blazer, I've put weight on since school, so we made our way back to our cabin to get an early night so as to be able to get up and watch us arrive in Stavanger early in the morning.....

Butter Watch.
It seems not everyone is familiar (where the heck have you been) with exactly what Butter Watch is. Well I shall endeavour to explain ⚫ First off, it's not the same as Winter Watch/Autumn Watch, there's no Chris Packham/Michaela Stracken on board, and no requirement for a Rab coat. Butter Watch is a very simple yet effective way of evaluating the consistency of our most favourite yellow spread. It was born in the autumn of 2021, onboard the magnificent Ventura, I was

upon my first cruise when I suffered a rather nasty incident on our first morning breakfast. I'd almost finished my full English, leaving only a lonely sausage, a fried egg and the baked bean juice. I'd requested 2 slices of toast, to make myself a nice sandwich to accompany me to the top deck to munch on whilst whale 🐋 watching. The toast was now only luke warm, and the butter was sat waiting patiently in it's little dish for it's moment. What happened next, is something that will live with me and those present for the rest of our day's. I carefully pushed the aforementioned remaining component's to the side of the plate and placed a slice of toast upon the cleared section. I took my right arm, and picked up the butter knife, not knowing what was about to happen. I attempted to guide the tip of the knife into the top knob of butter, that was staring longingly up out of the dish. And then it happened. The knife, bent like it was competing in the pole vault at the Olympics. Unfortunately, with no friction between the butter and bowl, something had to give. The butter 🧈 took off like a scud missile. My world entered a ' ' matrix ' like slow motion moment, as the lurpak launched across the restaurant. It was travelling at such speed it left a yellow vapour trail, and I'm certain created a sonic boom. It's trajectory took it straight, bang centre, into a lady's face, she was sat so happily enjoying her eggs benedict. It hit with such force that her head moved like one of them bobble heads that folk place in the back of car's. Before, gently sliding down her forehead, slipping like a sledge down the bridge of her nose, eventually lodging itself into her cleavage. Now ordinarily, as I'm very much a gentleman, I'd have offered to remove it and help clean up, but Helena was present, as was the lady's rather large and intimidating looking husband. So I just bowed my head down as if nothing had happened, and made my sarnie without butter.

At lunch of the same day, I proceeded with more caution when the butter arrived, and thankfully, the only issue I encountered was the bread roll I buttered tore itself apart, the evening meals butter was perfect, spreading like Debbie, the girl who ' did Dallas '

So thereafter, I started to rate the butter on it's hardness/spreadability, using famous people to rate it, eg. Dwayne ' The Rock ' Johnson/ Rambo would be hard/top of the scale, Tom Cruise/Pheobe Buffet mid level with Louis Walsh/Mary Poppins at the soft end of the scale, with more ' Utterly Butterly/ I can't believe it's not butter ' spreadability .

For your benefit, and to save you from any mishap/embarrassment, I've devised a small test you can undertake.

Take a plate, and place on the floor, just in front of your feet, approximately 4 inches, or 18 inches away if you're a porker. Then collect 1 knob of butter, and from waist height (dwarfs, head height) , drop knob onto plate. If the plate smashes, then I don't need to tell you, you ain't spreading it, it's only going to cause you misery. If the plate survives, but the butter retains it's shape, then it's borderline, use at your own risk. If when it drops, it changes shape, you're winning at life, and any bread/rolls/baps will still resemble themselves once the butter is spread upon them. Should the butter splat, and liquefy, then it's not fit for purpose, just discard carefully, don't drop it on the floor, it's very much a slip hazard.

Vegans, unfortunately I am unable to offer this service to yourselves as I'm soya and all that other crap intolerant, but please feel free to scale your own and add to the comments section, I'm very much a lover of all cultures, race and orientation ●.... one love ♥

Disclaimer :- If the wonderful lady whom was hit by the butter in the aforementioned incident shouldhappen upon this post, I take ABSOLUTELY no blame, Pam and Ozzy source the butter, it's not my fault that it was from the planet Krypton ●

Breakfast :- Tom Hardy (no pun intended)
Lunch :- Ed Sheeran
Dinner :- Kylie Minogue (perfection ●)

Slept like a baby last night ● Actually, no, NO I didn't, as babies don't actually sleep, they tend to scream all night long, and require constant attention !!! Stupid saying really !!! Slept like a bear ●, tho I did my business in the toilet, not the woods, be a silly thing to do now the back, sac and crack issue is clearing, wouldn't be nice squatting on a stinger !!!
Breakfast in the buffet this morning, and keeping with the bear theme, when ' Goldilocks ' took herself off to the bathroom, I quickly demolished her porridge, as I couldn't be bothered to queue up again ● blamed it on

the waiter ● not sure the aftermath later will be pleasant, mixed with black pudding and last night's horlicks, it's probably best I find the wood's and do as a bear does.

Today was our first port of call , Stavanger, and it was absolutely hammering it down. Like an idiot I forgot my kagoul, luckily for me, Helena had had her dress dry cleaned prior to the cruise (after an incident at a pineapple party last cruise) and she had left it in the plastic cover to protect it, I'm glad she did, made for the perfect substitute, kept me dry, all be it looking like a prat.

After my morning stroll, I met up with the others up in the crows nest. As it was the first day of contact with the outside world, my phone, once I turned off airplane mode literally exploded with notifications, and 100 missed calls from the kid's, apparently nobody wants to pick up the dogs lawn sausages ● . I threatened them with logging them out of my uber eats / deliveroo accounts, that seemed to bring them down to earth, tho I still imagine I'll have a poo mountain to see to upon my return... o the Joy's. For the record, the kids at home are 17, 19 and 25, with 2 of them having partners living with us and one of the dog's belongs to them, and it's an absolute machine when it comes to delivering his decking decorations!!! I expect the dishwasher is empty, and the work surfaces/sink full !! To calm myself down, and Helena; the missed calls wound her up no end, I decided I'd tinkle with the ol' ivory key's on the bar's grand piano. I soon realised tho, that I'm more penis than pianist, Elton John has nowt to worry about .

Lunch was taken at the Quays, it was absolutely rammed in there due to the weather, the biggest queue was for the KFC chicken 🍗, typical as this is what I fancied, so to slim the queue down, I rather loudly announced to Helena, intent on all hearing, that as we're now in Norway, the chicken wasn't chicken, but puffin and seagull, worked an absolute treat ⚫

Sail away was busy on deck, we decided to watch from the hot tub, lovely and warm, but crikey was it chilly on exit... you know the song 'I Left My Heart In San Francisco' , Well 'I left my balls in Iona hot tub' ⚫ Back at the cabin, I asked Helena to help me find em again, she was having none of it !!! A man can try ⚫

Captain had yesterday announced that we would be departing earlier than scheduled, 3 hour's earlier, due to a change in the weather and the sea conditions, a 2 metre swell was incoming and he wanted to make it out into open water, so as we could stick to the planned itinerary and make Olden as planned which I'm glad of, as it's the port I'm most looking forward to, I wanna build a snowman ⛄, I'm saving a carrot 🥕 from dinner especially ⚫

Before dinner, we (I was dragged) went to the shops again, specifically Pandora to purchase the £1 to make £45 must have cruise ship charm to add to the double dozen she already has, we tend to collect one that is synonymous with where we are/where we've been/what we've done. There's an apple 🍎 from our trip to New York, a shamrock ☘ from a Dublin vist, and a dummy for Amsterdam, was the closest thing to a butt plug ⚫

Dinner was in Coral tonight, we were sat right at the back, in the window, absolutely fantastic place to sit and dine, watching the waves dance 🌊 and it was a lovely meal, and lovely company from the adjoining table. What I like about the service here, is nothing is too much trouble for the waiter's, I'm often undecided with the course's, especially the starter and pudding, so I often get brought a few of the options ⚫ I'll see a whale 🐋 by the end of the cruise when it stares back at me from the mirror 🍴 ⚫

The ol' fella wasn't feeling the best after dinner, so he and my mother took themselves of to bed whilst Helena and I just wondered around exploring the ship some more, before finally giving in to our tiredness, we both want to rise early to watch the journey into Olden. I'll bet my all that only one of us will make it up on deck for sunrise and it won't be her.....

We did however grab a late (ish) night snack and horlicks each to take back to the room, we're so rock n roll ⚫

Butter Watch :-
Breakfast :- Rod 🥐
Lunch :- Jane 🥐
Dinner :- Freddy 🥐

And a new entry
Supper :- any Blue Peter presenter of your choosing.....

Today was port 2 day, the wonderful Olden, very scenic and very cold this morning. I shifted myself out of the warm bed at about 5.45 am, wanting to see and record our passage into and down through the Fjord. Back in blighty, I tend not to dress my age (according to the kids) I'm still somewhat a chav/roadman in my appearance, but I fit in very well here in the cold, rocking my North Face jumper and coat combo with my Timberlands. I completed the look by getting bally'd up and donning a pair of black gloves, i looked quite the mugger, but at least I was relatively warm, it was showing as minus 3 on my phone, and was raining/sleeting/snowing. As beautiful as the sail through was, I was a little bit disappointed. I didn't see a single Ford Capri, Grandma, Cortina or Sierra RS Cosworth !!! Was the same in Amsterdam, never once seen a hampster. I'm cancelling our bank holiday to Cockermouth and sending a strongly worded email to the Atlas writer's, it's a flagrant breach of the Trade Descriptions Act !!! After about half an hour, the weather made the visibility pretty rubbish, so I took myself back off to bed for a few hour's, much to the annoyance of Helena, to be fair to her, I probably should have took my wet gear off first ●

For breakfast we went down to opal where once again I opted for the full English, Helena taking it easy with just a yogurt and a crossiant. Now day to day life back on dry land, I never eat breakfast, I normally snack throughout the day, and have a dinner when I'm home, but when cruising, I'm eating like it's going out of fashion. Unfortunately, like what goes up, must come down, what goes in must come out !! And this morning's

' dropping the kids of at the pool ' was (no other way to describe it) Biblical, if I'd got signal inside the cabin, I'd have been calling Norris McWurter (probably brown bread now) to ascertain if it was a potential record breaker !! Like Loch Ness has a monster, I have delivered the The Fjord Mess Monster. I've also a new found respect for women 🙌, an epidural would have been well received 👍

Well and truly emptied, I felt good about getting off the boat to see what was about locally, I did wanna go to the Sky Lift, but the weather wasn't in our favour, and if honest, I didn't want to re mortgage just to be able to pay for it, why are Scandinavian countries so expensive? ⚫ I was also intending to have a wild swim today, but I'd forgotten to put my speedo's on, and I'm not up to speed on Norwegian laws when it comes to skinny dipping, so I'll save the swim, my dignity and wife's embarrassment until my return here in the summer ☀️

Back on board we headed to the buffet for a late lunch, I however got myself into a spot of trouble. As I mentioned yesterday, I wanted to ' build a snowman ⛄ ', well I didn't get to, i did however ' ride a bike around the hall ', I forgot to return it to the hire company, they called security, they unfortunately wouldn't ' let it go '

Sail away from Olden I have to say was a bit special, truly breathtaking if truth be told, I spent the evening filming a time-lapse of our transit back to the North Sea over a 4 hour period, having half hour break for dinner at the buffet, witness to an absolutely stunning sunset, but froze my tits off, was blowing a gale up on deck

19....glad I did it though, but by golly I was knackered, very long ass day...... out like a light once I hit the sac 🔴

Butter Watch :-
Breakfast :- Thor
Lunch :- Fred from Scooby Doo
Dinner :- Ed Sheeran
Are you worrying your life away, fearing a toast massacre at breakfast?? Settling for marg because you're fearful of carnage when attempting to butter your bloomer ??
Or worse still, going in dry??? Your bowl of minestrone doesn't deserve that.... neither do you. Not here and now on this cruise. Not on future cruises. Not at the Toby Carvery breakfast. Not ever.......
Fear no more....
Don't ' dread the spread '
ButterMan is ready to save the day....
Coming to all good cinema's (and crap one's) February 30th 2024... (need a few months to write the script)
Staring :-
Benedict Butteredbatch as our Saviour ButterMan (Tom Cruise not available due to filming Misson Impossible 29)

Charleze Spreadon as Marg A Rine our hero's arch nemesis

Directed by Steven Soderbread

Musical score by Spread Sheeran

So a little different start to the blog today, thought I'd throw my idea out to you lot first, I'm hopeful you'll be kinder than those in ' The Dragons Den ' 🐉 .. those of you who are kind may get to star as an extra ⚫
I got the idea while waiting for Helena to get sorted for the day. She'd got the TV on, and Doctors was showing. What the actual (insert your own expletive here) is that all about !!!! It's the most cheese thing I've ever seen, and I once had a cheese stuffed crust, only cheese pizza 🍕 at Cheddar Gorge. Now can I please let all know, that this is not in any way, shape or form, true to life of Birmingham, take it from me, the most Brummie brummie ever ⚫
I've already had many on here say I should be an author and write a book, well why walk when you can run ? 🏃 pointless just putting the tip in ⚫ If somehow the movie fails, then I will likely write a book 🎬

Alesund was today's port, and after breakfast I went out for an explore on my one's, Helena was " absolutely not in a million years " walking up to the observatory with me. So I grabbed my Karrimor gear and off I trekked, following the masses that had the same idea. At base camp, the trousers I'd chosen were quite a snug fit, but by the time I'd scaled the 416 steps up, they were a perfect fit, I must have burnt a few thousand calories. The views were quite spectacular, tho plenty of Ethel

Mermans kept walking past me while I was trying to take a selfie, their ship was docked behind ours. Annoyingly they cleared out the cornettos from the spar shop up top too, I had to settle for a funny foot ! Coming back down was an absolute breeze. Inspired by a video I'd seen last week, posted by passengers of Iona, who'd seen base jumpers in Olden. I'd took the quilt out of it's cover from our cabin before i set off, and holding each corner tightly I took the leap of faith, and like Mary Poppins, glided gently back down to terra firma. If anyone managed to video this epic act, I'd love to see it ●
I was well and truly ready for lunch ● after my expedition, so met up with the others at The Quays for fish and chips ● haddock today, and it was banging, much better than Harry Ramsden....
Had contact from home, daughter no.2 had dishwasher issues, she showed me the error code via video call, it was an F code, which is either F#%ked or Filter. As it's not very old, I assumed filter, so told her to pull it out and show me. It looked like a badly packed kebab/punched lasagne!!! Clearly nobody had been clearing the plates before putting them in. Looks like they'll have to go old school and wash up in the sink if they don't sort it.
Dad duties done, I got back to relaxing and, managed a few lengths in the pool, hopefully get a few lengths in later too ●
Part of what both me and Helena love about cruising ⛴ is people meeting, and this cruise, like those previous, pretty much everyone onboard are so friendly, I've also been inundated with friend requests on Facebook, more than happy to accept ●

Evening meal was tonight spent in coral restaurant, 3 courses are on offer, but I tend to have 5/6, tonight was no different 🌑 one of the starters was gravalax, but even after watching the advert where a guy in a restaurant is offered it, but hasn't a scooby, I was the same, so I didn't risk it. I went for 2 starters, a bowl of soup with some very nice foccacia and iberecio ham croquettes. I followed that with slow cooked pork collar steak in a mustard sauce, served with a mushroom and spinach roulade. Desert was a rather lovely lemongrass and coconut panacotta, and I couldn't resist the treacle pudding with sauce anglaise, dunno why they don't just call it what it is, custard 🌑 All being well I'll deliver another monster bog log, does anyone know if the onboard pharmacy stock gas and air ?
Butter Watch :-
Breakfast :- Sloth (The Goonies)
Lunch :- Gloria Estefan
Dinner :- Ronnie (F#@king) Pickering
Late Supper :- Salmen Rushdi

🔺 Word of warning 🔺
Long post today, sit tight, enjoy the ride.

Hi-de-hi campers, we're almost done, the finishing line is in sight 🌑 and that makes me very sad 🌑 back to reality for the majority of us I'm sure. Well luckily for you, I'm hoping to send you on your merry way with a smile on your face, I'm delivering a double dose of my rambling's, a brace of my sea faring adventures, a double dip, one in the pink- one in the sti.... !!!! No, I'll leave that analogy (pun intended) brings back that frightful misplacing incident on the Bay of Biscay 18 months ago.....

A little choppy sailing through the night and we arrived safely 🙌 at our final destination of Haguesund.

I woke fairly early from my slumber so took myself off alone for a breakfast for one. I changed it up a bit today, I refrained from the usual full English and opted for the egg's benedict. I was (as was my belly) very happy with my choice. They arrived beautifully presented on the plate, looking like Taylor Swifts delightful (I'd imagine) diddies. Firm but delicate, staring longingly up at me ⚫. As I buried my head into them, I mean gently burst them with my knife, the yolk oozed out in slow motion, like lava from a volcano, they were absolutely on point. Whenever I try to poach an egg 🥚 I'm left with what you'd usually find in a teenager's sock !!!! I finished off breakfast with a couple of fresh crossiants and a lovely cup of coffee ☕. I then headed of back to the cabin, where sleeping beauty still lay, she must have been warm, as she'd kicked the blanket off, for a minute, I thought I was still at breakfast, with my egg's benedict ⚫ I woke her up with a drink, I threw a glass off water 💧 over her ⚫. Safe to say she wasn't impressed!! But it had the desired effect, she quickly got up and dressed ⚫, we then took ourselves out together for breakfast ⚫, wasn't my place to tell her I'd already dined ⚫. Helena went for the Taylor Swift ⚫ I had the full English ⚫

Decided that we wouldn't get off today, my aching bones from yesterday's hike could do without further punishment, and I'll likely need the energy for tomorrow, I'm going to try and beat my previous sprint 🏃 record down the corridor of deck 11, fingers crossed nobody opens a door on me, had that happen on MSC virtuosa last year, and I was sub 9 seconds ⚫

Keeping with the theme of the week, when not off the ship, we like to chill in the crows nest, very peaceful up here and absolutely stunning panoramic view's. As it's not summer yet, upon the sundeck can be cold, especially on a sea day. I expect when we sail Arvia in October around the Mediterranean, we'll catch the sun up top most day's.

We didn't have an official lunch today, obviously no surprise there, I'm convinced I'd be a good match for @ Leah Shutkever with the amount of food and calories I've taken on each day this week. I think I'll have to top the air up in the tyres of the Allegro when we get back. Helena spent her time doing a cross stitch, myself I did a little work, had a few emails to reply top, and some jobs to order. I then took to Facebook and created ⚫ my new page, dedicated to my blogging, so if you're not already joined, then you know what to do ⚫ My sCRUISE loose, link below (probably a mile down by the time you've scrolled through all this ⚫)

It's during this relaxing time that I set my mind into gear and start my blogging, jotting down my garbage, in readiness to pen it later when I go to bed, I take an age to doze off, so I make use of the quiet time and type away, longer posts tend to coincide with Helena washing her hair or having a headache etc ⚫

Afternoon soon turned into evening, and we again dined in Coral, it's the biggest of the MDR's and is at the back of the ship with 180° view's out to see from the amazing panoramic double storey windows. The dinner was my favourite of the week, I started with ' sausage and duck liver in puff pastry, red pereronata and pine nut dressing ' - basically a posh Greggs sausage roll. Had cauliflower soup and pesto croutons with it 🦆. My main was ' roast pheasant breast served with cauliflower cheese, lemon and parsley stuffing, château potato, buttered greens and a pan gravy '... simply devine. For pudding I had ' baked New York cheesecake with a raspberry coulis, followed by the ABSOLUTE STAR of the show, a sumptuous ' warm chocolate praline fondant served with honeycomb ice-cream ' ...sensational 🦆.... I pity the toilet tonight.

Before hitting the sac, we popped up to the buffet for a horlicks and a hot chocolate, and in doing so, Helena found a hidden duck 🦆 how awesome 🔥

Thank you Fenwick Family.

Friday, final full day onboard and a sea day. I'm certain the pheasant I had last night thinks it's ' a phoenix ' only instead of resurrecting from the flames it's making a rather hasty departure through and out of my body to it's very final resting place, the ships septic tank, it's duty done, I'll remember it with fondness. I pondered skiping breakfast, but yesterday, I touched base with home, I spoke with my son's fiance about sorting me a new diet and fitness regime (she's very into that as a dancer) for me to start upon return, so one final max out ain't gonna hurt. So service as per, me the full shabootle, Helena on the poached egg's, tho this time on toast, not muffins. I also learnt of a toast tip, to late for me today, I'll try on leaving day. They only do DOORSTEP TOAST, just request, and the thickest toast at sea will soon arrive. A amazing thing for me today was my server. If anyone is a Friends fan (we are) you may remember the episode with ' Joeys Hand Twin ' 🍷 🍷, well, it wasn't a hand twin we had today, and it wasn't any way twin related to me or Helena. It was only a mustache twin to Freddie Mercury, the greatest entertainer to ever grace this earth ⚫ ' long may he reign ' ' there can be only one ' .... all being well I'll grab a selfie with him tomorrow, and let him know that he should feel privileged ⚫ at having such perfect top lip hair 🔥

When onboard, there's often announcements from the bridge giving updates, usually our location :- eg 20° east south west at a latitude of whatever at 16 knots, 100 nautical miles off theDutch coast.. just tell us we're in the middle of the North Sea, and there's no icebergs around to hinder us ⚫ much easier for us non sailors to understand..

Today has once again, you guessed it, been a crows nest day, I've been gazing out the window with my binoculars, seeing if I can spot any red light ladies with their baps out, considering were hugging the Dutch coast it's not beyond the realms of possibilities, these pringle tube binoculars are pretty good ⚫... just my luck, fog spoilt my chances, so dolphin and whales were the more likely spots, I've not seen any of those yet, a first, especially dolphins for me on a cruise, I'm usually very lucky have witnessed many, always thrills me ...

With lunch approaching, it was due time for my daily evacuation of the sewer spud. As we weren't at the cabin, one of the public kazies was of the order. The closest gents was out of service, so I had use the disabled/baby change one. Now the toilets on here have a self opening door. Great, as in the men's, and I'm assuming the ladies, there are individual cubicles. Not so great in these bogs, took me a while to figure out how to lock it, ● u pass your hand over a sensor that activates the lock, but pass over it again and the door opens. Be sure no bumblebees enter as u do, as the sensor is very sensitive. Thankfully I did manage to figure it out, a red light illuminates with a successful lock. Unfortunately, this wasn't the only issue I faced in here. Mid North Sea ● it appears Posiden has failed, like many local councils up and down the country, in keeping his roads, (shipping lanes in this instance), pot hole free. Mid crimp, i was ejected from my throne as we hit a crater sized one, and landed arse down on the lino, leaving a rather long smear, not unlike in appearance to those on the plates when they serve desserts on in the MDR !!!! One less wipe required...

Afternoon.... as it's the last day, that means 2 thing's. Packing, not my thing, happy to watch as it's done, I never do it correctly anyway, screwing it up into a bundle is " not how it's done " apparently. The single most important thing on final day however is........ shopping !! So for the umpteenth time, my sorry ass was dragged around every shop, where every perfume was smelt, (can you overdose on chanel no.5 ? I know you can on opium ●). Jo Malone was the chosen one, I thought, bit was quickly corrected, this was the woman from Shameless, apparently that's Tina, her fat sister 🍑 .... Obviously a bag was next, apparently a lady can never have enough, I reminded her of the draw full of ' bag's for life ' we have in the kitchen, not cutting it, so my wallet took another hit, tho I'm thankful it wasn't the first bag she'd looked at, a Mulberry one at an eye-watering £1200 !!! Add those to the Pandora charm and rings 💍 (got my mom one too) that were purchased earlier in the week, I think she's done OK 👍 Guess who's not getting the Brietling ....

Purchases done, as a non drinker, I drowned my sorrows with a triple scoop ice-cream from Ripples 🍦 bloody lovely 😋

Evening meal was spent in coral restaurant.

It's very much the busiest of the MDR'S, so I'd assume the best. Service is always 👌 bang on, and the food has been consistently excellent. As an MDR the dress code is smart, but that doesn't mean you have to boot and suit each night you want to dine here, with the exception of celebration night, smart casual is suitable with shoes. There's definitely a few in there of an evening trying their hardest to hold on to their youth, I'm no exception, but I think the leather look or silk clunge hugging trousers should remain on those under 30 unless you happen to be Elizabeth Hurley 💜, the only exception to the rule, if she somehow manages to see this, I'm on MSC Virtuosa 26th August, feel free to come along, preferably with a pineapple 🍍 🤎 🤎 🤎 🤎 🤎 ...... a man can dream 🤎 ... For my final dinner of the cruise I had a chicken satay starter, a sumptuous duck breast served with confit duck, green beans, savoy cabbage and a 5 spice infused jus, very tasty. Desert was a limoncello panacotta with a raspberry and orange coulis, another excellent dessert....

The evening finale was the show under the sky dome, the theme was birds 🦃 and have to say, was pretty good 👍. It was then a trip to the casino 🎰, this is now a tradition on our last night, we set a total spend of £20, gambling is not something we do, but it's a nice little end, especially if we win, unfortunately we didn't this time, our previous cruise we left with a win of just over £100 from our £20 spend.

A final trip to the late night buffet for a hot chocolate 🍫 and a dirty doner, tho no pittas, a cob has to make do, but it's as good as my local chippy. There was also coq au van on offer, Helena was tempted, but it reminded her of a not so pleasant evening in the back of my Ford Transit, bloody handbrake slipped, therefore so did I ⚫.......

And just like that, it's time for bed 🛌, an early night so as to get a final early brekky........ 💤 🍎 💤 🍎 💤 🍎 💤

Thought that was the end, but no... just before lights out, cabin phone rings, reception calling. Helena had left her bag up in the buffet, thankfully it was handed. Our thanks to whomever handed it over 🙌, I've already mentioned previously how nice people are on a cruise ship, this is further proof that we're all one big happy family 👥

Butter Watch :-
Slightly different today. These last 2 days the butter has been good to soft 🧈 So I'm rating it as a whole.
I'm dedicating it's glorious perfection to our Charlie, just in time for his coronation.

GOD SAVE THE KING 👑

And they all lived happily ever after......

THE END... ???
🖤 🖤 🖤

⚫ booooo ⚫ not fair ⚫ absolutely gutted it's over ⚫ I suppose ' all good things must come to an end '.
Very busy at breakfast this morning, was like Oxford Street on boxing day, seems everyone wanted their fill and be able to leave on a full tummy. To be fair to the staff, they managed the situation very well and efficiently, we were seated within minutes. Took it easy myself today, decided to leave one egg off my usual order and only 4 coffees ⚫ don't like unnecessary bog stops when driving home.
Then popped up to the buffet to grab a dozen boiled eggs, 6 pastries, 3 muffins, 4 baps and some bacon 🥓 to make me a light snack for the journey home. Used my pringle tube binoculars to store it all it. Also grabbed a few Kippers, managed to stealth drop them into the pocket of the guy who pushed past us into the lift last night, that'll teach him ⚫

Back to the room one final time, where thankfully I managed a final toilet transaction. A final check of the room left me a little disappointed with Helena, she'd missed packing 2 toilet rolls, 2 pillows, the TV remote and the hangers from the wardrobe !!! To late now !! Left a tip for our room steward, 2 of the egg's I'd got at the buffet (couldn't fit them all in the tube) and the cherries 🍒 from the haribo tangfastics I'd got in my pocket from journey here.

Disembarking the ship was very smooth once we were found, we'd tried hiding under one of the sofa's in the main atrium, but were spotted by a fellow passenger who was hiding a duck for the next sailing (I'm buying myself a duck fancy dress for next cruise, I'll slip into that on last day and hide out)

We were off and reunited with out luggage within 20 minutes, and easily passed through nothing to declare with our 10000 fags and 18 bottles of gin ⚫. Not so lucky was ' kipper in pocket ' guy, he'd found the kippers, and due to his manner, he wasn't happy, he got pulled to the side by customs, hopefully he got the full cavity search ⚫

We exited the terminal into the taxi rank, which was rammed, this seemed the most disorganised part of the disembarking, but was still pretty quick at 20 minutes and cost us just £7 to get us to the car, which was thankfully still there, minus it's wing mirrors and a smashed sunroof, which was soon fixed by wedging the smaller suitcase into the gap, sealed it with the rind from the bacon.

Driving home was pretty crappie, the bacon seal wasn't the best and it was absolutely chucking it down, it was almost like we were sailing again, especially when I aquaplaned. For dinner we stopped off at the services. We had Burger King 👑 , seemed befitting for the Kings coronation. It wasn't what i'd ordered, i don't order, I'm not made of money. What I do is clock those ordering at the screen, make a note of their order number, wait a few minutes before informing them that someone has just reversed into there car ⚫ off they run to check, their order number is called out, and bingo, free lunch ⚫

Our journey home chat was mainly focused on what would be left of our home and which of the kid's had /hadn't done this/that etc and who'd be the first to as " what you bought us " . As if by telepathy, the phone rang as we were pulling into the street, oldest son asking how long we'd be as there was no bog roll left !!! No sooner than I'd parked up, the youngest son was at the gate asking what we'd bought him !!! At least the house was still standing, recycling hadn't been put out for the binman tho, and there was significantly more on the pile, there was a pizza box mountain and maccie d's wrappers strewn across the garden. Dog's went absolutely mental when they seen us, weeing all over my Timberlands, and tripping Helena over, thankfully the recycling ♻ broke her fall. Once inside we were greeted by the sweet stench of day's old kebab remnants, stale vape and what looked like the washing up from the Last Supper 🍽. Like a true gentleman, I left Helena too it and took off to Asda for the bog roll, and sourced dinner

for us all from the markdown section ● quorn snack
eggs with slimming world tikka masala and a snapped in
half baguette, egg custards for pudding.
Knackered and sad, we had an early night. As a thank
you for an amazing holiday, Helena said I could ' go on
top ' ● disappointingly, she meant the top bunk !!! Still, I
was happy to be reunited with my memory foam pillow
and the Sky remote.

So, that's it for the blog. If you've enjoyed, I've created a
dedicated page so as the snowflakes can live their
mundane existence without my interference, I'd be most
grateful of your company and I'll be posting my previous
blogs there and my up and coming trips, just 111 day's
until I'm back on the sea :-) Link below.
There will be a full review from me, and I'll be penning a
serious post (yes, I can be normal lol)
Love to you all, I hope your sailing was perfect, your
journey home a safe one.
I look forward to meeting some of you onboard one day.
My upcoming cruises will be added to my page :-)

Serious post alert 🔺
Yup, you read correctly, a serious one.
Many of you have read my posts and have on the whole
enjoyed my humour. Well my humour and your support
of my rambling's and positive comments have been my
medicine, a sort of escape. Recently, life hasn't been so
kind and this trip was very much in doubt. My beloved

Helena was unfortunately in the very scary depths of a mental breakdown, so low in fact, suicidal, she could see no light from the darkness that had consumed and surrounded her.

This had massive knock on effect throughout the house, us all struggling to take it in, someone so very dear to us feeling like there was no point in living makes you question yourself too. What's hard with that is it can bottle up, as you don't want to cause more distress and despair. Luckily for me, I'm my own boss, so I was able to be there for Helena and our children when needed, and was very active in pro active change for us all, making the changes that would see her through to the light. We managed to get a new doctor onboard (no pun intended) who has quite simply SAVED HELENA'S LIFE. I'm happy to report that this cruise was part of the medicine and therapy needed, to further illuminate the once dark place. We are by no means at the end of this journey, but are moving further forward day by day, occasionally there's a bump in the road, but onwards we move. My rambling's/drivell, whatever you want to call it, are my own ' escape plan '

So, once again I thank you all, the joy you give me back with your kind comments and the fact I bring smiles to those who could well be where we are/were, drives me on..... with that, I sign off this post, and offer my inbox/my page as open to anyone who needs a shoulder, a cruise tip, or a laugh 🌑 to you...... it's good to talk....

Live... Love.... Laugh.....

O, and cruise xxx

Well, I suppose it's about time that I fulfilled my duty to you all and review my Iona experience.

First impressions, very similar to my beloved Helena's on our wedding night, " its huge ". The ship is the 10th largest in the world as I pen this, and an absolute marvel of engineering. Upon our arrival at Ocean Terminal I was a little miffed as to the absence of Pam and Ozzy. It's likely they were intentionally avoiding us, still embarrassed at our knowledge of the ' Black Pearl/Jack Sparrow/Pineapple ' incident that led them to cancelling our October trip to the Caribbean. O well, we weren't going to let it spoil thing's. We were sailing with my Mother and Stepdad, and as he is in a wheelchair, we were ushered through the special assistance entrance, bypassing a rather large queue. This gave us a very reasonable carpark to onboard in 25 minutes, seamless. Once on, as we were on different decks, we went our separate way's to seek out our cabin. This was our 5th cruise in 18 months, our very first in an inside cabin. We were on deck 11, room no.11324, so we made our way from the atrium to a lift. Lift swiftly arrived, full. Waited for the next one, yup, full again. 3rd time lucky, sort of, it was pretty full, but I squeezed us in, creating a little more space once doors were closed by letting out a silent arse biscuit, unfortunately it was a bad one, left us all gagging and seeking escape at the first floor the doors opened on. Fortunately for us, it happened to be deck 11. We were located mid fwd port side, so obviously went down the starboard corridor towards aft. 10 minutes of walking, we realised our error and turned around and eventually got to our room. Room found, and it was perfect, not the shoebox Helena envisaged. We also met with our steward Ben, very pleasant and helpful. Our cases had already arrived, so, as all good husbands do, I left her to unpack whilst I went exploring. Unfortunately, I didn't get very far, I forgot my carabiner's, and walking boot's were in the case's, so I took the moral high ground and helped her put the stuff in its home for the week, carefully scooping the case's contents up in my arms and depositing on the bottom of the wardrobe, kicking the empty case's under the bead. Wardrobe doors took a bit of closing, but all in all, job done well. That done, we'd worked up an appetite, so we put the exploring on hold and went in search of some fodder. Prior to the trip, we'd YouTubed our way through many hour's of videos, one of the place's we were keen to seek out was the Quays. Pretty much street food, with 3 separate diner's, one serving fish n chips, one serving Asian inspired dishes and a burger bar. Well I was like a tramp on chips, like an episode of Man Vs Food, I made my way through all on offer, all very good, but with all the eating on offer, there's consequence, you'll be like a lumberjack with all the logs you'll be chopping. There's also the buffet to get your quick food fix, morning, noon, afternoon, evening dinner and supper. You'll not starve on this ship. For the best included dining, then head to the MDR, food is fabulous, very masterchef in presentation, but without Greg Wallace, we chose Coral as our go to, nowt against the others, just ' better the devil you know ' after night one, ticked all the boxes so remained our goto. If you're lucky, you may get served by Oddjob from Goldfinger, we had him a few times, unfortunately he didn't have his hat, would have been great for cutting the crusty cobs.

Our celebration night was night 2, and it's a favourite of ours and many on the ship, a chance to put on your finest bib n tucker, for the mutton to dress as lamb, the James Bond wannabes. Five courses on offer this night. As a now seasoned cruiser, I'm clever on this night, I bring my ' stripper ' tuxedo, once the food baby starts making it's appearance, I just gently release a little of the velcro. Unfortunately (for me as a none drinker) there's free champers for all, I thought this was pop, and was tipsy by the 4th course, i must have thought I was on a ' stripping ' job due to the attire i was wearing, I was up on table 517, whipping of my gear like Magic Mike, gyrating in front of a group that included a couple of elderly, but very eager and up for it old dears, one got very friendly as I poured the amuse-bouche down my torso. Safe to say Helena wasn't happy, if there was a sofa in our room that night I wouldn't have been on it, I'd have taken both grannies ● any port in a storm.

Plenty of things to do on board, always something going on. You can take it easy in the library, relax in one of the countless hot-tubs. There's swimming, there's a gym, great for burning of the countless calories. There's a sport's arena out on the top deck, and u can even get your swing on, with either golf clubs or a pineapple 🍍
●

Of course a big draw for cruise ships is the entertainment on offer, some magical shows, brilliant comedian's, magicians 🎩 you may even be really lucky and bag a show with Gary Barlow, unfortunately our on offer celebrity was the very underwhelming Joe McElldry ⚫ I'd much have preferred Rage Against The Machine ⚫ No offence, he's no Olly Murs/Stacey Solomon ⚫ Our adventure took us to the beautiful Norwegian Fjords, and they were truly stunning, especially still covered in a winter blanket, tho a word of warning, Scandinavian countries are insanely expensive, and disappointingly there's no Earling Haaland statue, Ronaldo has loads in Maderia, so come on Norway, pull your finger out....

Shopping onboard is very much like shopping at an airport, you'll likely be sucked in buying stuff that will cost you far less back on land, I was, tho to be fair, it was our anniversary, so I thought I'd treat her to a Pandora. Should have bought her the GHD hair products, she was ' doing her hair ' EVERY night of the trip silly ⚫

We're both non drinkers, so didn't opt for a drinks package. Pay as u go drinks are in line with pubs on shore, in fact, I'd say a little cheaper, more in line with Wetherspoons price's ⚫

So would i/we recommend this ship ? Absolutely 100% as we would the itinerary. And for what I paid, less than £900 for the 2 of us for the week!!! Absolutely astounding value for money. I'm now looking forward to sailing on her sister ship Arvia in October ⚫

Almost forgot to mention.....
Butter ● think that Pam and Ozzy got the message from my 2 previous trips on Ventura.... it's pretty bang on now 80% of the time ● I just hope it's not utterly butterly/I can't believe it's not butter/flora in disguise

To

lovely to have met you.

Safe Onwards Journey & here's to many happy future travels x.

Much love

Mark Brady + the Crew xx.

Printed in Great Britain by Amazon